Abbott and Costello

THE CLASSIC COMICS

Compiled and
Edited by
TOM MASON

Malibu Graphics, Inc.

ABBOTT & COSTELLO
The Classic Comics
Volume One
Published by Malibu Graphics, Inc.
1355 Lawrence Drive #212
Newbury Park, CA 91320
805/499-3015

Printed in the USA
First Printing

Softcover
ISBN #0-944735-17-7
$14.95/$18.95 in Canada

Hardcover
ISBN #0-944735-18-5
$29.95/$37.95 in Canada

Abbott and Costello / compiled and edited by Tom Mason
p. cm -- (The Classic Comics: v.1)
Collection of illustrated stories from the Abbott and Costello comic book
ISBN 0-944735-18-5: $29.95 ($37.95 Can.)
ISBN 0-944735-17-7 (pbk.): $14.95 ($18.95 Can.)
I. Mason, Tom 1958- II. Abbott and Costello (Comic Book) III. Series
PN6728.A18A24 1989
741.5'973--dc20
89-32810
CIP

HEY ABBOTT!

Introduction by Tom Mason

Abbott: Who's On First?
Costello: Yes.

For more than four decades, Bud Abbott and Lou Costello were recognized comic masters—the stars of stage, screen, television, and comic books.

Comic books?

You betcha!

In the late '40s and early '50s comic books enjoyed a boom period. In the post-World War II era, paper was no longer as scarce as it once was leading to a resurgence of publishing in general (including the rise of the paperback original—a subject for another day). Comics were still selling at pre-war prices—10¢ a pop—and circulations hovered at the one million mark for successful titles. What better way to keep Bud Abbott and Lou Costello in front of their audience between pictures (which could take a year at a time) than a monthly comic book of their nutty adventures?

It was a practice used by several comedians of the time: Jackie Gleason had his own comic book from two different companies (*Jackie Gleason*—2 issues in 1948, 5 issues in 1955—and *Jackie Gleason And The Honeymooners*—12 issues, 1956-1958); Dean Martin and Jerry Lewis had their own series (*The Adventures Of Dean Martin and Jerry Lewis*, 40 issues, 1952-1957). When the duo broke up, Lewis got sole custody of the comic for another 84 issues (1957-1971); Bob Hope's title, *The Adventues Of Bob Hope*, ran 109 issues from 1950-1968.

The *Abbott & Costello* comic book had a healthy 40 issue run from 1948-1956 (including a 3-D comic in 1953—the height of 3-D mania). The series ended in 1956, coinciding with the break-up of Abbott and Costello and the demise of St. John Publishing with the death of its owner, Archer St. John. After the break-up, Lou Costello made several solo appearances before his death in 1959. Abbott retired, returning only to provide his voice for a series of Abbott and Costello cartoons in the '60s. He passed away in 1974. The *Abbott & Costello* comic book was revived in 1968 by Charlton Comics for an additional 22 issue run, lasting until 1971.

Comic books like these have certain limitations. With the absence of sound effects and music, overlapping dialogue, vocal inflections, tight editing, and non-stop slapstick motion, it's difficult to recreate Abbott and Costello's onscreen antics. It's one of the reasons that, with the exception of *The Wistful Widow Of Wagon Gap* (" A rip-roarin' story in four big rootin' tootin' shootin' parts") from the first *Abbott And Costello* comic, no further attempts were made to adapt their movies to the printed four-color page.

Another drawback to the stories in this collection is the lack of writer and artist credits--a tradition among comic book publishers of the '30s, '40s, and '50s and a headache for historians. Mort Drucker is the only creative talent who signed some of his own work (and whether he was allowed to or snuck it by the publisher isn't known). An exquisite draftsman and caricaturist, Drucker would eventually achieve fame and (together with fellow artist Jack Davis) set a house style for MAD Magazine that remains today, more than 30 years later.

No continuity between the stories is ever attempted. In one episode, they may be bungling private eyes (as in "Too Many Dummies" and "Private Eyes In Public"), then in military service (a popular setting for many post-war adventures, represented here by "Taken For A Ride") or just trying to enjoy a day at the beach ("The Octopus"). Other occupations include lion tamer, orchestra leader, and wrestler (check out Li'l Lou's headlock in "Terror Of The Mat").

As always, their personas, developed and honed to razor sharpness on stage and screen, remain essentially the same. Costello is the bungler, the prankster, the joker, getting both he and Abbott into all sorts of trouble. Abbott continues his role as straight man, bemused and somewhat annoyed by Costello's predicaments, yet quick to capitalize on the situation with a scheme to make them a fast buck (or so he hopes). Costello is the easiest to identify from panel to panel. His round, squat body and baby face made him a natural star for comics— he carries the bulk of the wild action and facial contortions. Abbott, as in the movies, gets the short end of the artistic stick. With his bland features and average build, he tends to get lost in the comic shuffle, reduced to sardonic comments with the occasional "Look out!" thrown in for good measure.

Despite its original run of 8 years and 40 issues, no mention is ever made of the comic book series in any Abbott and Costello reference book. How the series originated (although it's easy to guess since the first issue was an adaptation of their current movie) or how much control (or lack of it) was exerted by the principals, their agent, or the movie studio are stories unrecorded.

These comics are the product of a bygone era. The old stars like Abbott and Costello, The Three Stooges, Bob Hope, Martin & Lewis did everything and anything to keep their name and visage in front of the public— radio, television, stage shows, product endorsements, toys and games. It's hard to imagine today's comedians like Eddie Murphy and Steve Martin licensing themselves to comic books for additional exposure and money. They have, in a sense, bigger fish to fry.

Though they may be gone, Abbott and Costello continue to influence popular culture. Set in a monastery, an episode of the television series *Remington Steele* concerned the Abbott of Costello. "Who's On First?" is still in use today, particularly when describing poor business management. And, finally, Abbott & Costello movies (and their short-lived tv show) continue to play on television stations around the country.

So, sit back and relax. Pull this book off the shelf, or the coffee table, or the clothes hamper and curl up with one of the funniest and most popular comedy teams in history. You won't be disappointed.

ME AND THE BOYS

Foreword by S.A. Bennett

I come by my love of Bud and Lou naturally enough. My father never quite left 1942 and I inhaled his nostalgia like second-hand smoke. On Sundays we listened to an FM station that played "Golden Age of Radio" programs— big band music interspersed with episodes of *Jack Benny* and *The Lone Ranger*, *Gangbusters* and *Abbott & Costello*. And through the steady diet of b&w B-movies on our local UHF stations I was introduced to a monochromatic wonderland where cars had running boards and *everyone* wore hats.

I had an insatiable appetite for *Andy Hardy*, *Charlie Chan*, *Sherlock Holmes*, *The Bowery Boys*...and *Abbott & Costello*.

I was a lonely little boy who couldn't seem to do anything right, and Bud and Lou became close personal friends of mine. I followed them all over the world, from the arctic to the wild west, over and over again (I secretly suspected the station programmers were pocketing 90% of their budgets as I saw the same two dozen films between ages eight and eighteen) and could always depend on them...to be less competent than me.

One of the problems with having a higher education is you feel compelled to reconcile your love of art and literature with the childhood pleasures you cling to. I strongarmed my college film society into showing *Abbott & Costello Meet Frankenstein*, claiming that it was an example of the "explosion of genres" (a term I picked up in my film class). But it's foolish to try and make The Boys out to be more than they were— comedians who made funny movies.

The most gratifying thing for me is to know that I'm not the only one who remembers them. They've joined that select group of 20th century figures (W.C. Fields, Chaplin, The Marx Brothers, etc.) who've gone from being *people* to become *icons*. "Who's On First?" has entered the language and "Abbott & Costello Meet..." is the set up fon an endless number of jokes. Decades after their deaths, Bud & Lou can be seen flogging a high fiber cereal. But the litmus test of their continued popularity is, no voice over announcer has to say "Abbott & Costello for..." People know who they are.

I only wish there were *more* Abbott & Costello movies. I wish I could set my VCR for 4:00 AM and catch *Abbott & Costello Meet King Kong*, or *Abbott & Costello Vs. The Thing*. But I comfort myself with the fact that I can watch *Abbott & Costello Meet Frankenstein*...over and over again.

But beyond their films, their television and radio shows, I will always love them as cherished childhood companions. I don't care *how* stupid that sounds. I only hope you feel the same way.

S.A. Bennett is the creator/writer of the short-lived Rovers *comic book. He currently writes* Shuriken *for Eternity Comics.*

Other books by Tom Mason

SPICY DETECTIVE STORIES
A classic collection of seven two-fisted 1930s pulp detective stories from the pages of ***Spicy Detective*** *magazine.*

SPICY MYSTERY STORIES
Eight tales of mystery and suspense from **Spicy Mystery** *magazine of the '30s.*

THE THREE STOOGES
Nyuk! Nyuk! Nyuk! Those knuckleheads are back in this collection of seven slapstick adventures, including adaptations of "The Three Stooges Meet Hercules" and "The Three Stooges Go Around The World In A Daze."

DINOSAURS FOR HIRE
At last! A sensitive tale of teen-age angst and the trauma of growing up in middle class America. Just kidding! It's really about Dinosaurs with automatic weapons.
Illustrated by Chuck Wojtkiewicz and Terry Pallot.

Malibu Graphics, Inc.

DAVE OLBRICH • Publisher

CHRIS ULM • Editor-In-Chief

MICKIE VILLA • Associate Editor

TOM MASON • Creative Director

Cover Coloring: Bruce Timm

1: The Ape
originally appeared in *Abbott & Costello* #38, May 1956

9: The Octopus
originally appeared in *Abbott & Costello* #38, May 1956

16: Last Straw
originally appeared in *Abbott & Costello* #38, May 1956

20: The Man Without A Head
originally appeared in *Abbott & Costello* #38, May 1956

26: Terror Of The Mat
originally appeared in *Abbott & Costello* #38, May 1956

31: Up In The Air
originally appeared in *Abbott & Costello* #35, January 1956

35: Private Eyes In Public
originally appeared in *Abbott & Costello* #35, January 1956

44: Too Many Dummies
originally appeared in *Abbott & Costello* #35, January 1956

53: The Semi-Private Eyes
originally appeared in *Abbott & Costello* #32, October 1953

61: The Big Brush-Off!
originally appeared in *Abbott & Costello* #32, October 1953

69: Water, Water, Everywhere...
originally appeared in *Abbott & Costello* #35, January 1956

74: Two Knights In A Daze
originally appeared in *Abbott & Costello* #9, February 1950

81: Abbott & Costello Discover America
originally appeared in *Abbott & Costello* #9, February 1950

86: Out In The Baa-aa-aad Land!
originally appeared in *Abbott & Costello* #9, February 1950

92: Taken For A Ride!
originally appeared in *Abbott & Costello* #32, October 1953

100: Seen But Not Heard
originally appeared in *Abbott & Costello* #9, February 1950

104: To Be Or Not To Be??? and **What's The Use?**
originally appeared in *Abbott & Costello* #9, February 1950

105: The Model Male
originally appeared in *Abbott & Costello* #35, January 1956

107: Tropical Trappers
originally appeared in *Abbott & Costello* #23, January 1956

115: Tepee Town
originally appeared in *Abbott & Costello* #23, January 1956

120: Cover
originally appeared on *Abbott & Costello* #1, February 1948

121: Bent But Not Broke
originally appeared in *Abbott & Costello* #23, February 1956.

127: Man In Uniform
originally appeared in *Abbott & Costello* #23, February 1956

135: Groan And Bear It!
originally appeared in *Abbott & Costello* #23, February 1956

ABBOTT and COSTELLO
IN
"THE APE"
COSTELLO! I GOT A JOB IN A BROADWAY PLAY!
ATTABOY, ABBOTT! I ALWAYS KNEW YOU WERE A GREAT ACTOR!
ABBOTT and COSTELLO COMICS

NOW YOU'LL BE FAMOUS!
ER-.. NOT EXACTLY! AS A MATTER OF FACT, NOBODY WILL SEE ME!

NOBODY WILL SEE YOU? HOW COME?
I'M GOING TO BE WEARING AN ANIMAL COSTUME!

DON'T TELL ME YOU'RE PLAYING A HORSE?
NO! NO! NOT THIS TIME! I'M GOING TO PLAY AN APE IN "JUNGLE JUNGLE"!

AT LEAST IT'S A PART WHERE YOU'LL HAVE HAIR ON YOUR CHEST!
I'M GONNA PICK UP THE COSTUME NOW.

GOT TO GET INTO AN APE-LIKE MOOD!
?

MEANWHILE...
CIRCUS DELIVERIES

GRRRR!

BOOIINNG!

CIRCUS
DELIVERIES

THUD!

DID YOU HEAR A CRASH?
CRASH? NOPE... ER... MAYBE A THUD!

GRR-RR!
ULP!

HMM... ABBOTT LEFT HIS SCRIPT HERE!
I THINK I'LL PRACTICE TO BE HIS UNDERSTUDY!

GRR! UGH-H!! GRUNT!

GROWL!
?

GA-RUNT!!

Y'BACK, ABBOTT? I DIDN'T EVEN HEAR YOU COME IN!
?

BOY, THAT'S A REALISTIC LOOKING OUTFIT!
THUD!

GROWL!

WOW! WHERE DID YOU GET THAT GROWL?
YOU SCARED THE DAYLIGHTS OUT OF ME!

?

CRASH!

NOW WHAT DID YOU HAVE TO DO **THAT** FOR?

CRACK!

WHAT THE HECK IS THE MATTER WITH YOU, ABBOTT?

YOU BETTER TAKE THAT COSTUME OFF! I THINK YOU'RE **OVER-HEATED** OR SOMETHING!
?

ULP!

Y-YOU'RE A **REAL APE!**

HALP!

GOTTA GET OUTA HERE!

ULP!! THE CLOSET!
GR-RR!

OKAY, MOTHS... MOVE OVER!
SLAM!

KNOCK!
KNOCK!

G-GO 'WAY! TH-THERE'S NOBODY HOME!

I THINK I'LL SURPRISE COSTELLO AND PUT THE COSTUME ON IN THE HALL!

THIS'LL MAKE HIM JUMP, I'LL BET!

THIS OUGHTA BE GOOD! ≈CHUCKLE-CHUCKLE≈

A-A-R-OWRGH!
?

COSTELLO, WHERE DID **YOU** GET A COSTUME?
?

A-ABBOTT! TH-THAT AIN'T ME! **I'M** IN THE CLOSET!

THAT'S A **REAL** APE! I DON'T KNOW HOW HE GOT HERE!
WHAT?

?

GIVE ME BACK MY HEAD, PLEASE!

LET'S MAKE A DASH FOR IT, ABBOTT!

THAT'S NOT ME!
ULP!

THE APE CLIMBED IN THERE, MISTER!
THANKS, SONNY!

KNOCK!
KNOCK!
COME IN!

PRUNELLA! WHO'S YOUR FRIEND?

I'M NOT HER FRIEND!
HE'S APPEARING IN A PLAY!
OH!

I WAS DELIVERING HER TO A CIRCUS WHEN HER CAGE FELL OUT OF THE TRUCK AND BROKE OPEN!
PRUNELLA GAVE US QUITE A SCARE!
YOU AIN'T KIDDING!
PRUNELLA'S PERFECTLY TAME... NOTHING TO BE AFRAID OF!
NO?
WATCH THIS! YOU CAN EVEN SLAP HER IN THE FACE AND SHE WON'T DO ANYTHING!
SLAM!
SEE?
WHAM!
HMM... JUST GOES TO SHOW, YOU CAN NEVER TELL ABOUT APES! COME ON, PRUNELLA!
MORT DRUCKER
GROWL!! A-R-RGH! ROUGH! ROUGH!
NEXT TIME, SEE IF YOU CAN GET THE PART OF A GIRAFFE! THEY CAN'T MAKE A SOUND!
THE END

ABBOTT and COSTELLO
IN "THE OCTOPUS"
by MORT DRUCKER
WHAT A DAY! I CAN'T WAIT TO GET OUT ON THE BEACH!
FORGET IT! WE CAN'T GO!

HUH? WHY NOT?
WE CAN'T WEAR OUR BATHING SUITS UNDER OUR CLOTHES, 'CAUSE YOU'RE NOT ALLOWED TO UNDRESS ON THE BEACH!

WELL, LET'S GET A LOCKER AT THE BATH-HOUSE!
THAT WOULD BE FINE EXCEPT FOR ONE THING...

...IT COSTS TWO DOLLARS!
OUCH!

HOW ABOUT WALKING TO THE BEACH WEARING OUR BATHING SUITS?
NO GOOD! YOU'RE NOT ALLOWED ON THE STREET WITH JUST A BATHING SUIT!

HMM...LEMME SEE...

I HAVE IT!

QUICK! PUT ON YOUR BATHING SUIT!
BUT...
DON'T ASK QUESTIONS!

NOW WE TAKE A FEATHER FROM THE DUSTER AND THIS OLD NECKTIE...
?

...THERE!
WHAT IS THIS?

NOW, TWO BLANKETS!

WE'RE TWO INDIANS 'UST OFF THE RESERVATION!
BY GOLLY, THIS MAY WORK!

HOW!
HOW!
?
BEACH

?

INJUNS!

TAKE THAT, YOU REDSKINS!
HEY!
OUCH!

HERBERT! STOP THROWING THOSE STONES!
YOU'RE A BAD BOY!

AFTER MOTHER SPENT ALL MORNING GATHERING THOSE PRETTY STONES, YOU GO AND THROW THEM AWAY! SHAME!

HEY! YOU'RE NOT REAL INJUNS! YOU'RE A COUPLE OF PALEFACE BAD-MEN IN DISGUISE!

MISTER, CAN I PLAY WITH YOU, MISTER?
CAN I, HUH? CAN I?
GO BACK TO YOUR TV SET, WILL YA, KIDDO?

HEY, COSTELLO! YOU'RE SITTING ON THE SANDWICHES!

COSTELLO! I'M TALKING TO YOU!
HUH?

GET OFF THE SANDWICHES!
OH! I WAS WONDERING WHY THE BLANKET WAS SO LUMPY!

HI, SISTER!
HI!
?

HMM... HIS SISTER! IT MIGHT BE WORTH MAKING THE LITTLE BOY'S ACQUAINTANCE!
WHY DON'T YOU LEAVE WELL ENOUGH ALONE?

?
HEY, KID...

YEAH, MISTER. WILL YOU PLAY WITH ME, MISTER?
WILL YOU PLAY WITH ME?
SURE THING, LITTLE CHUM!

HOW ABOUT COVERING ME UP WITH SAND?
OKAY!
I'M GOING IN FOR A DIP!

TEN MINUTES LATER...
Z-Z-Z-Z-Z-Z!
HEY! THAT'S NOT FAIR... FALLING ASLEEP!

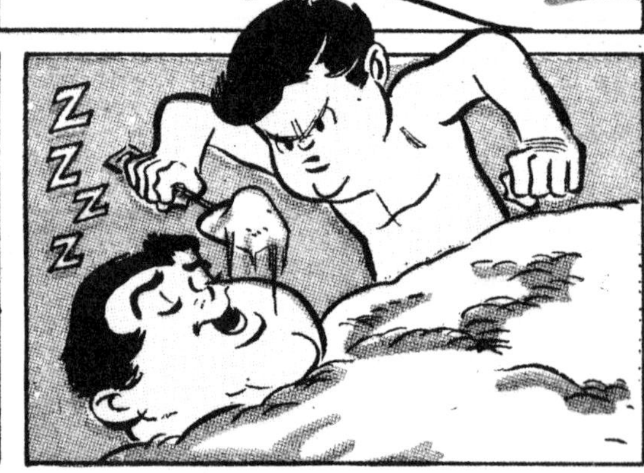
Z Z Z Z

HERBERT! GET THAT SHOVEL OUT OF THE MAN'S MOUTH! YOU'LL BREAK IT!

PTUIII!!
YOU SAID YOU WERE GONNA PLAY WITH ME AND YOU WENT TO SLEEP!

HAVING FUN, COSTELLO?
IF IT WASN'T FOR HIS BEAUTIFUL SISTER...

HEY... WHEN IS YOUR SISTER COMING BACK, KIDDO?
SISTER? WHAT SISTER?

YOU REMEMBER... THE GIRL WHO WAS PASSING! YOU SAID HI, SISTER!
OH, THAT WASN'T MY SISTER! I WAS MAKIN' LIKE A GANG-STER! AND GANGSTERS CALL ALL GIRLS SISTER!

HA! HA! HA! HA!
GRRR! I THINK I'LL GO IN THE WATER AND COOL OFF!
ME, TOO!

GO 'WAY, BOY! YA BOTHER ME!
AREN'T WE FRIENDS ANY MORE?

YA BETTER WATCH OUT FOR THE OCTOPUSES!
AH, YOU'RE JUST TRYING TO SCARE ME!

YIPES! OCTOPUS!
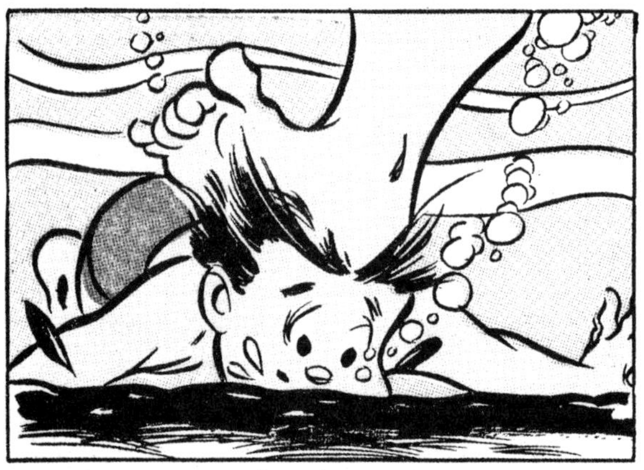

EE-YIKE! IT'S A SHARK!

HELP!

YOU!
BAW!

HERBERT! WHAT HAPPENED?
HE TRIED TO DROWN ME!
?

GOSH, COSTELLO! AFTER ALL, HE'S ONLY A KID!
BUT I DIDN'T... OUCH!
OGRE! BRUTE!

HEY, ABBOTT! WAIT FOR ME!
SCOUNDREL! NO GOOD!
GRAB YOUR BLANKET!

HOW!
HOW!
?
BEACH

FEET, KEEP MOVIN'!

WHEW! I THINK WE DITCHED HER!
PUFF-PUFF THAT WOMAN'S CRAZY!

THE NEXT TIME A KID SAYS TO ME...

MISTER, WILL YOU PLAY WITH ME, MISTER? HUH? WILL YOU, MISTER?

HELP!
The END

ABBOTT AND COSTELLO

in LAST STRAW

WELL, COSTELLO... NOW WILL YOU BELIEVE THAT IT'S ONLY A MIRAGE?

SINCE WHEN DO MIRAGES HAVE TEETH?

WHAT ARE YOU GOING TO DO WITH YOUR PART OF THE LOST PYRAMID TREASURE, COSTELLO?
GASP TAKE THE NEXT PLANE OUTA HERE!

ABBOTT, THIS CHARACTER AND ME DON'T SEE EYE-TO-EYE!
C'MON, COSTELLO! STOP HORSING AROUND!

THE ANCIENT EGYPTIANS BURIED THEIR KINGS WITH DIAMONDS, RUBIES AND GOLD...
I'D RATHER HAVE A FOAM RUBBER MATTRESS!

COSTELLO, HOW STUPID CAN YOU GET?
I DON'T KNOW! I AIN'T EVEN HALF TRYING!

I'M NOT GONNA GASP MAKE IT, ABBOTT!
SURE YOU WILL! JUST THINK WHAT LIES AHEAD OF US!

AND HALF OF IT WILL BE YOURS!
WHAT AM I GONNA DO WITH TWO HUNDRED MILES OF SAND?

C'MON, COSTELLO! A LITTLE EXERCISE CAN'T HURT YOU!
EXERCISE! THIS IS MURDER! BESIDES I'M DYING ... GASP WATER! WATER!

STOP BEING A BABY, COSTELLO!
STOP BEING A BABY? I WISH I'D NEVER STARTED BEING A MAN!

NOW LOOK WHAT YOU DID, LUNKHEAD! YOU SCARED OUR CAMEL! C'MON, WE'LL HAVE TO HOOF IT!

One hour later...
IF YOU HAD A CHOICE, ABBOTT, HOW WOULD YOU LIKE TO DIE?
I'D LIKE TO ≈GASP≈ DIE OF OLD AGE. WHAT ABOUT YOU?

I'D LIKE TO DROWN! BOY, THAT WOULD BE LIVING!
COSTELLO--LOOK! AN OASIS! WATER!

NOW WHO'S BEING A JERK? THAT'S JUST A MIRAGE!
YOU'RE RIGHT, COSTELLO! WE'RE WHACKY FROM THIS HOT SUN!

WE'RE SEEING THINGS!
YEAH... IT'S ALL IN OUR MINDS!

WE'RE JUST SEEING WHAT WE WANT TO SEE!

HEY, ABBOTT!! ≈GLUG...GLURG≈

THIS MIRAGE ISN'T FOR REAL, ABBOTT, BUT I'M GOING DOWN FOR FOR THE THIRD TIME!
OKAY, OKAY! JUST DON'T RUSH ME!

One narrow escape follows another...
WE'RE NEVER GONNA MAKE IT, ABBOTT!
DON'T GIVE UP! ACCORDING TO THE MAP, WE'RE NOT FAR FROM THE LOST PYRAMID!

LOOK, COSTELLO!
I AIN'T TAKING ANY CHANCES, ABBOTT! LET'S GO AROUND IT! THAT LAST MIRAGE ALMOST KILLED ME!

IT'S THE LOST PYRAMID! WE'RE RICH!
HEY! WAIT FOR ME!

ONLY A FEW MORE YARDS!
GOOD! GASP! I'LL DIE A WEALTHY MAN!

ULP!
WHAAA...?
LOST PYRAMID TOURS
TRIPS DAILY
LOST PYRAMID DINE
HAMBURGERS

...AND HERE IS A PERFECT EXAMPLE OF THE NATIVES OF THIS DESERT AREA...
THE END

ABBOTT and COSTELLO

IN

"THE MAN WITHOUT A HEAD"

COSTELLO, YOU'RE IN! I'VE GOT YOU A JOB HERE, TOO!

WILL I GET TO SEE THE CIRCUS?

POP CORN

BUT I *MEAN* IT! THE REGULAR PERFORMER IS SICK, AND THEY NEED A SUBSTITUTE!
AH, COME ON, ABBOTT, STOP KIDDIN' ME! WHAT DO I DO?

FIRST OF ALL, SEE THE RINGMASTER, AND TELL HIM I SENT YOU.
I'M OFF!
YOU CAN SAY *THAT* AGAIN!

MR. RING-MASTER, MY NAME IS COSTELLO! MY FRIEND ABBOTT SENT ME.
OH, YES! RIGHT THIS WAY, MR. COSTELLO!

THERE'S A UNIFORM IN THERE FOR YOU! PUT IT ON AND JOIN ME IN THE BIG TENT!
THANK YOU, SIR. ER...JUST WHAT AM I SUPPOSED TO DO?
LION TAME

DON'T WORRY ABOUT A THING! I'LL GIVE YOU ALL YOUR CUES!
OH, OKAY!

HMMM... NOT BAD!

HERE I AM, MR. RINGMASTER!
GOOD! YOU'RE ON!

JUST STEP INTO THIS CAGE!
THIS CAGE?

?
CLANK!

RRROAR

TH-THAT'S FUNNY! TH-THAT SOUNDED LIKE A LION!

YIPE! IT IS A LION!

YIII! LEMME OUTA HERE!

HA, HA, HA! LOOK, DADDY! THE LION TAMER IS PRETENDING TO BE AFRAID OF THE LION!
HA, HA, HA, HA!

FOR GOODNESS SAKE, COSTELLO, PULL YOURSELF TOGETHER! THAT LION IS AS GENTLE AS A LAMB!
I WISH IT WAS A LAMB!

JUST GO OVER TO IT AND SAY... "FLOSSIE! OPEN!"
FLOSSIE? OPEN?

F-FLOSSIE! O-OPEN!

ROARRRR!
YII!

YOU'VE GOT TO SAY IT WITH MORE FORCE, LIKE YOU'RE IN CONTROL OF THE SITUATION!
GULP OKAY!

FLOSSIE! OPEN!
YAWN!

NOW WHAT?
PUT YOUR HEAD IN!

WHAT? ARE YOU NUTS? THIS IS THE ONLY HEAD I'VE GOT!
YOU WANT THE FIFTY BUCKS, DON'T YOU?

IT'S PERFECTLY SAFE! I GUARANTEE IT!
YEAH! BUT DOES THE LION GUARANTEE IT!

ABBOTT SURE GOT ME A SWELL DEAL!
GOODBYE, BRAINS!

MR. RINGMASTER! THERE'S BEEN A TERRIBLE MISTAKE! THAT'S THE WRONG LION IN THERE!
EH? WRONG LION?

THAT'S NOT FLOSSIE! IT'S A NEW LION THAT HASN'T BEEN TRAINED YET!
OMIGOSH!

COSTELLO! STOP! THAT'S THE WRONG LION!
NOW HE TELLS ME!

ULP!
SNAP!

HALP!
USE YOUR WHIP!

ON GUARD!

HEY, LEGGO!!! THIS IS THE ONLY WEAPON I HAVE!

YIIII!!
SWISH!

KLUNK!

Meanwhile...
POPCORN!
I'M A LITTLE WORRIED ABOUT COSTELLO!
OF COURSE, THE LION IS WELL TRAINED, BUT...
I'D NEVER FORGIVE MYSELF IF THE LITTLE FOOL GOT HIS HEAD BIT OFF! I'LL GO SEE!

WHERE'S THE NEW LION-TAMER?
THEY CARRIED HIM TO HIS TENT!
POP CORN

CARRIED HIM?
YIPE!
LION TAMER
CIRC

COSTELLO! YOU'VE LOST YOUR HEAD!
I'LL NEVER FORGIVE MYSELF!
THIS IS TERRIBLE!

ABBOTT, STOP BABBLING LIKE AN IDIOT, AND HELP ME GET THIS COAT OFF! I'M STUCK!

OOPS!

COSTELLO, YOU'RE GONNA BE THE DEATH OF ME YET!
HMM! THAT'S A HOT ONE! I'M GONNA BE THE DEATH OF HIM!
THE END

ABBOTT and COSTELLO

in TERROR of the MAT

GET OFF THE FLOOR, COSTELLO! HOW ARE WE GOING TO MAKE MONEY WITH YOU IN THAT POSITION?

WE MIGHT NOT MAKE ANY MONEY, BUT LOOK AT THE REST I'M GETTING!

LI'L LOU

OH BOY! STEAK!
DON'T FORGET THAT SPINACH! AND DON'T TRY TO HIDE IT IN YOUR SHIRT LIKE THE LAST TIME!

NOW RELAX AND BE READY FOR THE SLAUGH--ER... FIGHT TONIGHT! IF WE DIDN'T NEED THE MONEY I'D NEVER LET YOU GO IN THERE AGAINST THE APE-MAN! BUT WE'LL BE BRAVE ABOUT IT!
WE WILL? YOU'RE MY FRIEND, ABBOTT!

HEY, ABBOTT! WHAT'S THIS LI'L LOU? WHAT AM I? A GIRL OR SOMETHIN'?
THAT'S PSYCHOLOGY, STUPID! WITH A NAME LIKE THAT, THE APE-MAN WILL THINK OF YOU AS A FAT, POWERLESS, LITTLE GUY!
TONIGHT
APE-MAN
VS
LI'L LOU

HEY! THAT'S TRUE! I'M GETTING OUT OF HERE!
WHAT? ARE YOU GOING TO STAND THERE AND TELL ME WE'RE SCARED?

WHO'S STANDING? ANYWAY, I DON'T KNOW ABOUT YOUR HALF, BUT MY PART IS A FAT, POWERLESS LITTLE GUY!
WELL, MY HALF IS BRAVE AND STRONG AND NOT SCARED OF ANY FER-OCIOUS APE-MAN.
DRESSIN
ROOM

TELL ME WHICH HALF IS YOURS AND I'LL LET IT DO THE FIGHTING!
OH, NO! YOU THINK I'M GOING TO GO IN THERE AND BREAK MY NECK AND LET YOU STAND BY? AS BUDDIES WE GOT TO GO IN THERE TOGETHER!

AWW... YOU'RE CUTE!
YOU GOT TO DO THIS IN WRESTLING. YOU'RE LI'L LOU AND I'M YOUR NURSE. IT'LL MAKE THE AUDIENCE REMEMBER US.

LI'L LOU-- YOU'RE ON IN FIVE!
OKAY, COSTELLO. HOP IN!
OH, BOY! A FREE RIDE!

SING
OM
ARGHH!
I GIVE UP! LET'S GO HOME!
DON'T BE SILLY! HE JUST LOOKS LIKE THAT TO SCARE YOU!

THE APE-MAN ...GOSH...WOW!
HEY, ABBOTT! CHATTER-CHATTER MY HALF M-MUST BE THE FEET. THEY K-KEEP WANTING TO RUN!
THEN STOP CHATTERING WITH MY TEETH!

C'MON, BUDDY! I HATE THIS AS MUCH AS YOU DO!
SURE, BUT THE WORST THAT CAN HAPPEN TO YOU IS, YOU'LL PAY FOR MY FUNERAL!

I KNEW THIS WOULD HAPPEN. THAT'S WHY I HAD THE CARRIAGE GIMMICKED!
HE-E-EY, ABBOTT!

ABBOTT SURE GOT ME ALL BALLED UP!
WELL, WHAT'CHA KNOW... A BOUNCIN' BABY!

MOIDER HIM! THROW DE BUM OUT!
AND NOW I LAY ME DOWN TO SLEEP!

ATTA-BOY, COSTELLO! BOUNCE BACK AT HIM!
NOW I KNOW HOW A TENNIS BALL FEELS!
TWAANNG

THAT'S MY BUDDY IN THERE!
?

WHERE ARE YOU GOING? YOU HAVE HIM ON THE RUN!
SURE! BUT HE'S RUNNING MY WAY!

HE'S HURTING MY HALF!
WELL, GET HIM WITH MY HALF!
HMM... VERY INTERESTING! VERY INTERESTING!
CRRASK!

ARGH! UGH! UGH!
HEY! NO FAIR TELLING SECRETS!
UGH! UGH!

NAUGHTY! NAUGHTY! YOU'LL HURT HIS FINGERS!
I'M SORRY! I'M A BAAAD BOY!

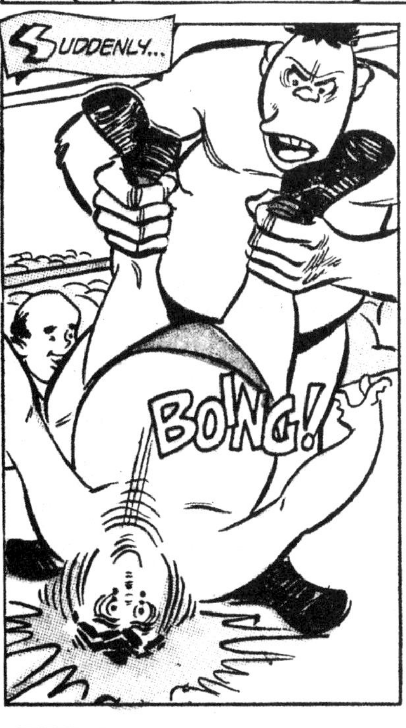
SUDDENLY...
BOING!

YOU WANNA GIVE UP, ABBOTT? THIS IS YOUR HALF HE'S HURTING!
NO! NO! NEVER! TICKLE HIS FEET!

HO-HO-HO! HEE-HEE!
MY KINGDOM FOR A FEATHER!

ONE, TWO, THREE, TICKLE! ONE, TWO, THREE, TICKLE!
HA-HA-HA-HA!

AFTER THREE TICKLES...
THAT'S MY PAL!
AH! NUTHIN' TO IT!
THE WINNER!

A FEW MOMENTS LATER...
SNIFF-SNIFF
GEE! THE POOR APE-MAN. I THINK I SHOULD SHOW HIM A TRUE CHAMPION AND GO OVER AND CONSOLE HIM!
ARE YOU CRAZY? DON'T DO IT, COSTELLO! I'M WARNING YOU!

UGH... WE SORRY... UGH... I... UGH... HEY! HOW DO YOU TALK TO AN APE?
DON'T FEEL SO BAD, OLD TOP! C'EST LA GUERRE! AND SUCH ROT! BUT WAIT! I HAVE A BULLY IDEA! GRAB HIM, TOGA!

NO, FELLA... NO! LEMME UP!

WAIT TILL OUR NEXT BOUT! I'LL BEAT YOUR SILLY BRAINS OUT!
HEY... HA! HA! HELP, ABBOTT! HA! HA! HA!
WELL... DIDN'T I WARN YOU?
THE END

ABBOTT and COSTELLO in
UP IN THE AIR

WOLE AIRCRAFT COMPANY

COSTELLO! WHAT ARE YOU DOING?

ME? I'M ENJOYING THE BREEZE! I JUST TURNED ON THE STARTER, AND LOOK-- *AIR CONDITIONING!!*

X 234

COME TO THINK OF IT, SO AM I! NOW WHAT KNOB DID I TURN TO START THESE THINGS?
X 234

MAYBE IT WAS THIS ONE...

COSTELLO! THE PLANE'S MOVING!
I GUESS THAT WASN'T THE RIGHT KNOB!
X 234

WE'RE HEADING TOWARD THE HANGER, LUNKHEAD! TURN THE WHEEL! PUT US IN REVERSE! HURRY!
YOU JUST HOLD ON TIGHT, ABBOTT! I'LL TRY AGAIN!

STOP IT, COSTELLO! STOP IT! WE WENT RIGHT THROUGH THE HANGER!
GOOD EXAMPLE OF LOW FLYING, WASN'T IT?

NOW WE'RE UPSIDE DOWN! YOU'RE TAKING TEN YEARS OFF MY LIFE!
DON'T FLATTER YOURSELF! TEN YEARS OFF YOUR LIFE AND YOU'D BE PUSHING DAISIES!

HELP! I'M GETTING DIZZY! CAN'T YOU STOP THIS THING?
SHE'LL STOP SOON. WE'RE RUNNING OUT OF GAS!

ABBOTT, WE'RE IN LUCK! I FOUND TWO PARACHUTES!
PASS ONE TO ME! I'M LOSING MY GRIP!

OOPS! IT'S COMING AT ME AWFULLY FAST!

YOU LET IT SLIP RIGHT THROUGH YOUR FINGERS. NOW WE'VE ONLY GOT ONE 'CHUTE LEFT!

LOOK, ABBOTT! IT'S GOOD YOU DIDN'T USE THAT ONE! IT DIDN'T OPEN!
NO ONE PULLED THE RIP CORD, STUPID! NOW GET THE OTHER 'CHUTE!

YOU MEAN WE BOTH FLOAT DOWN TOGETHER? DO YOU KNOW HOW TO OPEN IT?

SURE! IT'S SIMPLE! YOU JUST PULL THAT CORD!

THIS ONE? HMM! LET'S SEE...
NO! COSTELLO! NO!!

GOODY! IT WORKS! NOW WE'RE READY!

READY, MY EYE! NOW WE'RE REALLY STRANDED, YOU NINCOM-POOP! NOW PULL ME UP!

WHAT ARE YOU GONNA DO NOW, ABBOTT?
FLY THIS CRATE!

SEE HOW SHE RESPONDS TO MY TOUCH! SHE'S SLOWING DOWN!
NO WONDER! SHE'S OUT OF GAS!

COSTELLO! WE'RE GONNA CRASH!
IF I LIVE THROUGH THIS, I'LL ALWAYS KEEP MY FEET ON THE GROUND!

CRASH!

W-WHERE ARE WE? WHO ARE THOSE STRANGE PEOPLE RUNNING TOWARD US?
IT'S MR. WOLFE! HERE'S WHERE WE GET THE AXE!

FIRED? DON'T BE SILLY, BOYS! SUCH COURAGE MUST BE REWARDED! I'M PRO-MOTING YOU TO PERMANENT TEST PILOTS!
WE QUIT!
END

ABBOTT and COSTELLO in "PRIVATE EYES in PUBLIC"

WE CERTAINLY COULD USE A CLIENT. I WISH A CASE WOULD FALL INTO OUR LAPS!

SOCIAL REGISTER

HERE COMES OUR CASE NOW, ABBOTT!

KATCHEM-KWIK DETECTIVE AGENCY PRIVATE EYES NOSE & THROAT

WHAT HAPPENED? WHERE AM I? WHO AM I?
YOU CRASHED THROUGH OUR SKYLIGHT-- REMEMBER?

I DON'T REMEMBER A THING! NOT EVEN MY NAME!

WE'LL JUST CALL YOU REGGIE. WHAT WERE YOU DOING WITH THIS SOCIAL REGISTER?
SOCIAL REGISTER! THAT STRIKES A FAMILIAR CHORD!

I'LL READ OFF THESE NAMES AND. . . HEY! ABBOTT! LOOK WHAT I FOUND UNDER THE M'S!
MONEY!

THAT MONEY IS MINE!
A GREENBACK WILL BRING A MEMORY BACK EVERY TIME!

I REMEMBER HAVING THIS MONEY. BUT I STILL DON'T KNOW WHO I AM. IF YOU BOYS FIND OUT I'LL REWARD YOU HANDSOMELY!
DON'T WORRY IF YOU'VE EVER BEEN BORN, WE'LL FIND OUT WHO YOU ARE!

THERE'S AN OPEN WINDOW IN THE ROYAL ARMS APARTMENT HOUSE NEXT DOOR! MAYBE REGGIE FELL OUT OF IT!
ABBOTT I'M PROUD OF YOU!

WE'LL GO UP TO THAT APARTMENT. MAYBE SOMEBODY THERE KNOWS REGGIE!
LET'S NOT RUSH THINGS, ABBOTT. HE MAY WANT TO PAY BY THE HOUR!

IT'S THE CHIEF, HOIMON! HOW DID HE GET IN THAT BUILDING? AND WHO ARE THOSE GUYS WITH HIM?
I DON'T KNOW. BUT HE'S GOT THE SOCIAL REGISTER. YOU'VE GOT TO HAND IT TO HIM!

HE WAS LOOKING RIGHT AT US AS IF HE DIDN'T RECOGNIZE US! HE PASSED US UP!
YOU THINK HE'S GIVING US THE OLD DOUBLE-CROSS?

AND THOSE TWO GUYS HAVE GUNS! THE DIRTY DOG MUST HAVE GOTTEN A COUPLE OF KILLERS TO PROTECT HIM!
SURE! THAT'S IT! HE'S GOT THE DOUGH AND HE WANTS IT ALL FOR HIMSELF!

I'LL HAVE TO BE CAREFUL! IF THE CHIEF HIRED THEM YOU CAN BE SURE THEY'RE TOUGH KILLERS!
WE'LL TAKE THEM BY SURPRISE! WHEN WE GET INTO THE LOBBY I'LL YELL "NOW"! THEN START SHOOTING!

MY MEMORY'S STARTING TO COME BACK. I REMEMBER ENTERING THIS BUILDING AND THROWING THAT CIGAR BUTT THERE!

I'LL WRAP THE BUTT IN MY HAND-KERCHIEF AND THEN IF WE DON'T FIND OUT WHO YOU ARE, REGGIE, WE'LL EXAMINE IT FOR YOUR FINGER PRINTS!
"NOW"! HOIMON! "NOW"!

RUN FOR YOUR LIFE! THE FAT KILLER HAS EYES IN THE BACK OF HIS HEAD!
PLOP!

BE CAREFUL WITH THAT GUN, COSTELLO! YOU'RE LIABLE TO HURT SOMEBODY-- AND HURRY! WE'VE GOT TO GO UP!
Y-Y-YOU'RE RIGHT! LET'S GO!

THAT APARTMENT WITH THE OPEN WINDOW ON THE TWENTY-FIFTH FLOOR. PRESS THE BUTTON, COSTELLO!
I'M STILL A LITTLE NERVOUS. YOU'D BETTER DRIVE!

THEY MUST BE GOING TO BLEWBLODZ APARTMENT!
WE'LL GO UP THE FIRE ESCAPE!

HELP! ABBOTT! HELP! SOMEBODY'S GIVING ME A NECKTIE PARTY!
YOU FOOL! YOUR TIE'S CAUGHT IN THE DOOR!

AND WHEN THE ELEVATOR REACHES THE TWENTY FIFTH FLOOR.
MY NECK FEELS LIKE IT'S BEEN IN A TAFFY-PULL!
OH BE QUIET! THAT SHOULD BE THE APARTMENT THERE!

NO ANSWER! BUT THIS MUST BE YOUR APARTMENT, REGGIE!
RING! RING!
AND THAT PROVES YOU'RE NOT AT HOME!

BUT LOOK! THE DOOR'S AJAR! LET'S GO IN!

HOLEY SMOKES! THE BUBBLE GUMMERS MUST BE HOLDING A CONVENTION INSIDE!

THESE ARE THE SOAP BUBBLES AND THEY'RE COMING FROM THE BATHROOM!
SOME-BODY MUST BE USING THE LARGE ECONOMY SIZE!

THE BUBBLES ARE COMING FROM THAT CAKE OF SOAP!
NO SENSE IN LETTING ALL THOSE BUBBLES GO TO WASTE!

WE'RE ON A CASE REMEMBER!
SPOIL SPORT YOU!
I'D BETTER TAKE THIS SOAP OUT OF THE WATER!

WHAT BUBBLE DANCER DO I REMIND YOU OF?
NONE! NOW PUT THAT SOAP DOWN AND GET YOUR CLOTHES ON!

MEANWHILE, OUTSIDE ON THE FIRE ESCAPE . . .
BUBBLES AND MORE BUBBLES! I CAN'T SEE INSIDE!
THEY MUST BE COMING FROM THAT BUBBLE SOAP OL' BLEWBLODZ INVENTED!

THE BUBBLES ARE STARTING TO THIN OUT! I CAN JUST MAKE OUT THE FAT KILLER SITTING IN THE CHAIR!
WHAT ARE YOU WAITING FOR? LET HIM HAVE IT!

ABBOTT! WHATSAT?
BLAM!

QUICK! LET'S GET OUT OF HERE! THIS PLACE IS FULL OF MOTHS!

I'D BETTER SHUT THE WINDOW, I FEEL A DRAFT!

I DID! SEE ALL THOSE HOLES IN HIS CLOTHES? THE BULLETS HIT HIM BUT DIDN'T HURT HIM!
YEOW! I THOUGHT YOU SAID YOU GOT HIM!
HE MUST BE A SUPERMAN!

I'VE NEVER TANGLED WITH ANYBODY LIKE HIM! HE'S UN-CANNY! LET'S GET OUT OF HERE!
HE'S THE TOUGHEST KILLER I EVER MET BUT WE'LL GET A MACHINE-GUN AND COME BACK THAT'LL FIX HIM!

AND INSIDE THE APARTMENT . . .
LOOK! THERE'S A MOVIE CAMERA! IT MUST HAVE BEEN ON FOR HOURS TAKING PICTURES!
GOOD! LET'S DEVELOP THEM AND RUN THEM OFF! THEY MAY TELL ME WHO I AM!

THIS MUST BE THE DARK ROOM. WE CAN DEVELOP THEM IN HERE!
COULDN'T WE LIGHT IT UP? I'M AFRAID OF THE DARK!
OFF
ON

ALL RIGHT, COWARD! SEE! THERE'S NOTHING TO BE AFRAID OF!
ABBOTT! A BODY!

I WONDER WHO HE IS?
I DON'T KNOW HIM BUT HIS TOWEL LOOKS FAMILIAR. I TOOK ONE FROM THAT HOTEL MYSELF.
HOTEL MAJESTIC

'PON MY WORD! WHAT HAS HAPPENED TO ME, OL' BEAN? WHERE AM I, OL' THING? WHO AM I, OL' BOY?
THIS GUY HAS AN OLD ENGLISH ACCENT!

MOST PECULIAR! I CAWN'T REMEMBER A THING.

WE'LL DEVELOP THIS FILM! IT MAY SHOW WHO EACH OF YOU ARE.
RIGHT! ON WITH THE SHOW

FINALLY THE FILM IS READY TO BE PROJECTED.
EVERYONE READY FOR THE FEATURE FILM? SORRY, NO POPCORN AVAILABLE.

OOOH! I'M SCARED! THE BLACK HAND GANG IS MIXED UP IN THIS!

'PON MY WORD! I REMEMBER NOW! I HAD THE CAMERA TURNED ON TO MAKE MOVIES OF MY NEW BUBBLE SOAP IN ACTION WHEN THE DOORBELL RANG.

I ANSWERED THE BELL-- AND HE BOPPED ME!
REGGIE, WHAT MANNERS!

NOW I REMEMBER, TOO! YOU'RE BLEWBLODZ! I PUT YOU IN THAT DARKROOM. THEN I TRIED TO GET AT THAT DRAWER-- BUT IT STUCK!
SORRY, OL' CHAPPIE. I ALWAYS MEANT TO HAVE IT FIXED!

REGGIE I THINK THIS IS YOUR FINAL SCENE!
YEAH! THAT'S WHEN I FELL THROUGH THE WINDOW INTO THE OFFICE OF YOU TWO NIT-WITS!

I'M RED BADBLOD, THE NOTORIOUS KILLER! I KNEW BLEWBLODZ HAD HIS DOUGH HIDDEN IN HIS SOCIAL REGISTER AND I CAME HERE TO GET IT.
THAT WAS HARDLY CRICKET, OL' TIMER.

NOW I'M GETTING OUT OF HERE. ONE PEEP OUT OF ANY OF YOU AND YOUR PICTURES WILL BE IN THE OBITUARY PAGE.
ABBOTT, THAT MIGHT BE GOOD PUBLICITY FOR US WHY DON'T YOU PEEP?

WHAT! HEY! I'M SLIPPING! THAT ☆#% SOAP!
GET HIS GUN LOU!

GOT IT! NOW REACH FOR THE SKY! ABBOTT, CALL THE POLICE!
COSTELLO! I'M PROUD OF YOU!

A FEW MINUTES LATER THE POLICE ARRIVE.
WONDERFUL WORK, BOYS! HOW DID YOU CAPTURE HIM?
I'LL RECONSTRUCTICATE, CAPTAIN. HEY, ABBOTT, OUTTA MY WAY!

RED BADBLUD WAS TRYING TO PULL THIS DRAWER OUT-- BUT IT STUCK. SO HE PULLED HARDER AND HARDER--

AND WHEN IT CAME OUT-
SWOOSH!

MEANWHILE ON THE FIRE ESCAPE BELOW. . .
NOW THAT WE'VE GOT THIS MACHINE GUN, WE'LL FINISH THAT KILLER!

HERE HE COMES! HE MUST HAVE HEARD US!
DON'T HIT US! WE WERE ONLY KIDDING, KILLER!

AS COSTELLO FALLS THROUGH SPACE, HE HITS THE TWO THUGS, PUSHING THEM OFF THE FIRE ESCAPE. . . THE TRIO PLUNGES TOWARD THE BROKEN WINDOW OF THE KATCHEM KWIK DETECTIVE AGENCY

TWO MINUTES LATER.
LOOK! HE'S CAPTURED SPIKE KILLJOY AND NAILS MURDERSROW. BADBLOD'S HENCHMEN! WE'VE BEEN AFTER THEM FOR YEARS.
COSTELLO, ARE YOU ALL RIGHT?
WHERE AM I? WHO AM I? WHAT HAPPENED?
THE END.

Too Many Dummies

A C
DETECTIVE
AGENCY
ERTAKINGS

YIPES! A CORPSE!

NOT ONLY THAT-- BUT HE'S DEAD!

DON'T JUST STAND THERE, ABBOTT! INTRODUCE US!
DO YOU REALLY THINK IT'S NECESSARY?

THIS IS DEADLY ERNEST FISHER! I'M HIS WIFE-- BODY FISHER!
DEADLY ERNEST! THE GANG-STER?
YOUR MAMA SURE NAMED YOU RIGHT!

D-DID YOU KILL HIM?
DON'T BE SILLY! THIS ISN'T ERNEST-- IT'S JUST HIS TAILOR'S DUMMY!

DUMMY?
YES! I BROUGHT IT ALONG SO YOU'D RECOGNIZE DEADLY ERNEST WHEN YOU SEE HIM!
WHAT WERE YOU USING HIM FOR? A PIN CUSHION?

OH, THE KNIFE? I JUST PUT IT THERE TO SHOW YOU WHAT I WANT DONE TO HIM IF HE SHOWS UP!
WE'RE PRIVATE EYES--NOT KNIFE-THROWERS!

I KNOW! I WANT TO HIRE YOU TO PROTECT ME FROM DEADLY ERNEST! HE'S WANTED BY THE POLICE FOR A BANK JOB...

I SANG TO THE POLICE.
I WISH YOU'D SING TO ME. WE COULD MAKE BEAUTIFUL MUSIC TOGETHER.

DEADLY ERNEST ESCAPED THE POLICE DRAGNET, BUT HE SWORE HE'D GET ME.
OVER MY DEAD BODY ⁝GULP⁝ WHAT AM I SAYING?

THAT MUST BE DEADLY ERNEST'S HATCHET MEN!
DON'T BE SILLY! A HATCHET NEVER MADE A NOISE LIKE THAT!
A&C DETECTIVE AGENCY
BAM! BAM!

WE MISSED THE DOLL, BULLETS!
HOLY SMOKES! WE WINGED DE BOSS BY MISTAKE!
A&C DETEC

YOU KILLED HIM! YOU BAD, BAD BOY!
I-I GUESS WE NEED SOME TARGET PRACTICE!

WELL, THE LEAST WE CAN DO IS TO BUMP OFF THE DOLL!
AN' THESE TWO DOPES, TOO!

DON'T DO ANYTHING HASTY, MEN! THERE'S NO NEED FOR ANY MORE KILLING!

WHERE DEADLY'S GONE, HE'LL PROBABLY NEVER HEAR ABOUT IT ANYWAY!
I NEVER THOUGHT OF THAT!

BESIDES WE COULD HELP YOU GIVE HIM A BEAUTIFUL FUNERAL! I BET HE'D LIKE THAT!
SUCH TOUCHING SENTIMENT!
I'M GONNA CRY!

WE'LL PUT HIM IN THIS TRUNK... THEN TAKE HIM OUT TO SOME PRETTY SPOT IN THE COUNTRY!
IF HE WUZ ONLY ALIVE TO ENJOY THIS!

MAYBE WE SHOULD BURY HIM WITH ALL HIS BELONGINGS-- YOU KNOW, TOMMY GUNS, KNIVES, REVOLVERS...
YEAH! HE MIGHT NEED THOSE THINGS. WE'LL DRIVE BY HIS ROOMING HOUSE AN' PICK 'EM UP!

DON'T WORRY, DEADLY! WE'LL MAKE SURE YOU'RE COVERED IN CASE YA RUN INTO ANY OF MALLEY'S GANG UP THERE!
NOW YOU'VE DONE IT! IF THEY FIND DEADLY ERNEST ALIVE IN THAT BOARDING, HOUSE, WE'LL BE DEAD!
I-I NEVER THOUGHT OF THAT!

HEY--LOOK! THERE'S A COP!
DON'T STOP YOU TWO--OR YOU'LL STOP LEAD!

WHAT DO YOU FELLOWS HAVE IN THAT TRUNK?
JUST A LITTLE OLD BODY, OFFICER!

I HEARD YOU TWO WERE A COUPLE OF KIDDERS! A LITTLE OLD BODY--THAT'S A GOOD ONE!
HE DOESN'T BELIEVE US! NOW WHAT'LL WE DO, ABBOTT?

YOU! YOU ALMOST GAVE THE SHOW AWAY! I SHOULD LET YOU HAVE IT!
DON'T WASTE YOUR WARES ON ME, BOYS! I'M ON YOUR SIDE!

HERE WE ARE! I MAKE A MOTION THAT SLUG AND BULLETS RUN UP WITH THE TRUNK AND GET DEADLY'S STUFF!
I SECOND THE MOTION!/ ALL IN FAVOR SAY AYE!
SEASIDE HOUSE

NAY-NAY!
AYE!
NAY-NAY!
AYE!
AYE!

THE NAYS WIN--FOUR TO THREE! YOU GUYS GO UP! WE'LL WAIT HERE!
HE MUST BE A POLITICIAN!

AN' DON'T TRY ANYTHING FUNNY IF YA WANTA KEEP BREATHING!
WE WON'T!
PUFF-PUFF MY BREATHING'S RUNNING A LITTLE SHORT RIGHT NOW!

NOW WE'RE REALLY IN FOR IT!
DON'T WORRY! I'VE GOT AN ACE UP MY SLEEVE!

A LOT OF GOOD THAT WILL DO!
I'VE ALSO GOT A TEAR-GAS BOMB IN MY POCKET!

YOU OPEN THE DOOR, THEN I'LL THROW IN THE BOMB!
THEN WE'LL GRAB DEADLY ERNEST AFTER THE FUMES BLIND HIM!
2C

READY? ONE--TWO--
ABBOTT! I DROPPED IT!

BUTTERFINGERS! I MIGHT HAVE KNOWN YOU'D FOUL THIS UP!
SOB-SOB LET'S NOT CRY OVER SPILT TEAR-GAS!

WE'D BETTER WAIT DOWNSTAIRS TILL THE FUMES THIN OUT!

MEANWHILE, THE TEAR-GAS FUMES SEEP UNDER THE DOOR OF DEADLY ERNEST'S ROOM...
TEAR-GAS! THE COPS MUST BE TRYING TO SMOKE ME OUT!

WHEW... IT'S EVEN WORSE IN THE HALL! I'LL HIDE IN THAT TRUNK TILL THIS BLOWS OVER, THEN SHOOT IT OUT!

WELL, I'LL BE--! MY TAILOR'S DUMMY! HOW DID IT GET HERE?

I'LL TOSS IT IN MY ROOM AN'--

OUCH! MY HEAD!

SOB THIS SMOKE WILL NEVER CLEAR OUT! LET'S CREEP BACK UPSTAIRS AND GET THE TRUNK.
BOO-HOO GOOD IDEA. WE'LL TELL SLUGS AND BULLETS THAT DEADLY'S DOOR WAS LOCKED!

LOOK! DEADLY'S DOOR IS OPEN! HE'S LYING ON THE FLOOR!
HE MUST BE DEAD!

NO HEART BEAT! HE'S GONE ALL RIGHT!
WE'LL LEAVE HIM HERE AND GO TO THE POLICE AND TELL THEM THE WHOLE STORY!

THIS TRUNK SEEMS A LOT HEAVIER!
IT'S BECAUSE WE'RE A LOT MORE TIRED!

IT'S ABOUT TIME YOU GUYS SHOWED!
YEAH! WE SAW SMOKE UP THERE! WE WERE AFRAID YOU WERE COOKING SOMETHING!
WE COULDN'T FIND ANY GUNS OR KNIVES!

I'LL TAKE A LOOK INTO THE TRUNK TO MAKE SURE EVERY-THING'S JAKE!

WE'RE SUNK IF THEY REALIZE IT'S JUST DEADLY'S DUMMY!

POOR DEADLY! HE LOOKS SO PEACEFUL LYING THERE!
YOU'D ALMOST THINK HE WAS SLEEPING!
IMAGINE! THEY THINK THAT DUMMY IS REALLY DEADLY!

I KNOW A LONELY SPOT IN THE COUNTRY. WE'LL DRIVE OUT THERE AND BURY DEADLY!

TWO HOURS LATER...
HERE WE ARE! YOU TWO GET BUSY DIGGING A GRAVE. YOU'LL FIND PICKS AND SHOVELS IN THE TRUNK OF THE CAR!

GROOOAANN!
DID YOU HEAR WHAT I HEARD?

THIS PLACE GIVES ME THE CREEPS!
IT SOUNDED LIKE IT CAME FROM FROM THE TRUNK!
NO! IT WAS JUST AN OWL!

OWLS DON'T HOOT IN THE DAY TIME! IT CAME FROM THE TRUNK!
LET'S JUST BURY IT AND GET OUT OF HERE!

DEADLY'S GHOST HAS COME TO HAUNT US!
THE DUMMY'S COME TO LIFE!
I'M NO DUMMY AND NO GHOST! I'M THE REAL McCOY-- DEADLY ERNEST!

NOW I GET THE PICTURE! WELL, BODY, SAY YOUR PRAYERS. AND YOU TWO JOIN IN!
YOU'RE NOT GOING TO KILL US IN COLD BLOOD, ARE YOU?

NO. I'M GOING TO LET YOU FINISH DIGGING THAT GRAVE FIRST. THAT OUGHT TO WARM UP YOUR BLOOD UP A BIT!

YOU CAN START DIGGING NOW! MAKE IT DEEP ENOUGH FOR ALL THREE OF YOU!

I'M KINDA PLUMP! I'LL DIG JUST A LITTLE DEEPER. I WANT TO BE COMFORTABLE!

THOOMP!

WHEN THE SMOKE CLEARS...
HE SHOT US! WE'RE DEAD!
NO, WE'RE ALIVE! LOOK AROUND YOU!

THAT SURE WAS A SMART TRICK, MISTER, HITTING THAT GAS PIPE WITH YOUR PICK!
WHEN WE HEARD THE EXPLOSION, WE CAME OVER TO INVESTIGATE AND FOUND THESE CROOKS--OUT LIKE A LIGHT!
I DON'T HAVE WORDS TO THANK YOU!
HONEY-- THIS IS WORTH TEN THOUSAND WORDS! YUM-YUM!
THE END

ABBOTT & COSTELLO in The SEMI-PRIVATE EYES

KATCHEM-KWIK
DETECTIVE AGENCY
PRIVATE EYES, NOSE & THROAT

A DAGGER FLIES THROUGH THE AIR TOWARD ABBOTT AND COSTELLO, BUT DOES THIS INTREPID PAIR FLINCH? YES... WHAT CRIMINAL, WHOM THEY BROUGHT TO JUSTICE, IS OUT FOR REVENGE? ***NONE...*** THEY NEVER HAD A SINGLE CASE! THEN WHAT IS THE ANSWER?

GRADE A

I AM MRS. BUCKSINBANK. HERE IS A HUNDRED DOLLARS AND IF YOU DO YOUR JOB WELL, THERE WILL BE ANOTHER HUNDRED.
I DIDN'T KNOW THIS KIND OF MONEY STILL EXISTED!

WHY, WHAT'S THE MATTER WITH IT? CONFEDERATE DOUGH?
DON'T MIND HIM, MA'AM. WHAT CAN WE DO FOR YOU?

A HUNDRED DOLLARS! OOHH!! THIS IS MORE THAN MY POOR HEART CAN STAND!
COSTELLO! PULL YOURSELF TOGETHER OR I'LL PULL YOU APART!

I'M GIVING A MASQUERADE PARTY TONIGHT. I'LL BE WEARING MY FAMOUS "HOPELESS DIAMOND." YOUR JOB IS TO BE SURE NO ONE STEALS IT!
AREN'T YOU AFRAID OF GETTING ROUND-SHOULDERED WEARING THAT ROCK AROUND YOUR NECK?

COME IN MASQUERADE COSTUMES, THEN NO ONE WILL SUSPECT YOU OF BEING PRIVATE EYES!
YOUR WORRIES ARE OVER. WE'LL GUARD THAT DIAMOND WITH OUR LIVES!

OH! SOMEONE FOLLOWED ME HERE! QUICK!! IS THERE ANOTHER WAY OUT?

SURE! THIS DUMB-WAITER LEADS TO THE BASEMENT CAFETERIA...
AND SEND ME UP A SANDWICH, WILL YOU?

ALL RIGHT, YOU TWO! WHERE'S MRS. BUCKSINBANK?
SEARCH ME! BUT BE GENTLE-- I'M TICKLISH!

SO! SHE WENT THIS WAY! WHAT DID SHE WANT?
SHE WANTED US TO GUARD HER DIAMONDS AT HER MASQ--
SHUT UP, YOU BLOCK-HEAD!

IF YOU VALUE YOUR HEALTH, YOU WON'T GO TO THAT PARTY! YOU'LL FORGET YOU EVER SAW MRS. BUCKSINBANK!
Y-YOU CAN'T SCARE US!!

NO? WELL THIS IS A SAMPLE OF WHAT YOU'LL GET IF YOU SHOW UP THERE TONIGHT.

SLAM!
S-STOP SHAKING, C-COSTELLO! NOW THAT HE'S GONE, WE'D BETTER GET OUR COS-TUMES FOR THE PARTY!
I THINK WE BETTER RECONSIDER THIS WHOLE DEAL!

I GAVE MRS. BUCKSINBANK OUR WORD WE'D BE THERE. AND AN ABBOTT NEVER GOES **BACK** ON HIS WORD.
WELL A COSTELLO NEVER GOES ***FOR-WARD*** ON HIS.
MAS
COST

WE HAVE NOTHING TO FEAR NOW. THE MASKED MAN WILL NEVER SEE THROUGH OUR DISGUISES.
IF HE DOESN'T, HE'LL BE THE ONLY ONE!
MASQUERADE COSTUM
FOR ALL OCCASIONS

THAT NIGHT, AT THE BUCKSINBANK MASQUERADE PARTY...
DON'T WORRY, MRS. BUCKSINBANK. THE ONLY WAY A THIEF COULD PINCH YOUR DIAMOND IS OVER OUR DEAD BODIES!
THAT'S WHAT I'M AFRAID OF!

HEY, ABBOTT! SOMEONE TURNED OUT THE LIGHTS!
MAYBE MRS. BUCKSINBANK DIDN'T PAY HER LIGHT BILL!

HELP! MY DIAMOND! HANDS OFF, THIEF!

I'VE GOT HIM, ABBOTT!
I'VE GOT HIM, COSTELLO!
SOMEBODY TURN ON THE LIGHTS!

WHEN THE LIGHTS WENT ON...
YOU!

MY HOPELESS DIAMOND! IT'S GONE!!

BUT I DID MANAGE TO GRAB A HANDFUL OF HAIR FROM THE COSTUME OF THE THIEF!
THAT HAIR IS FROM A LION'S MANE! NOW LET'S FIND THE LION!

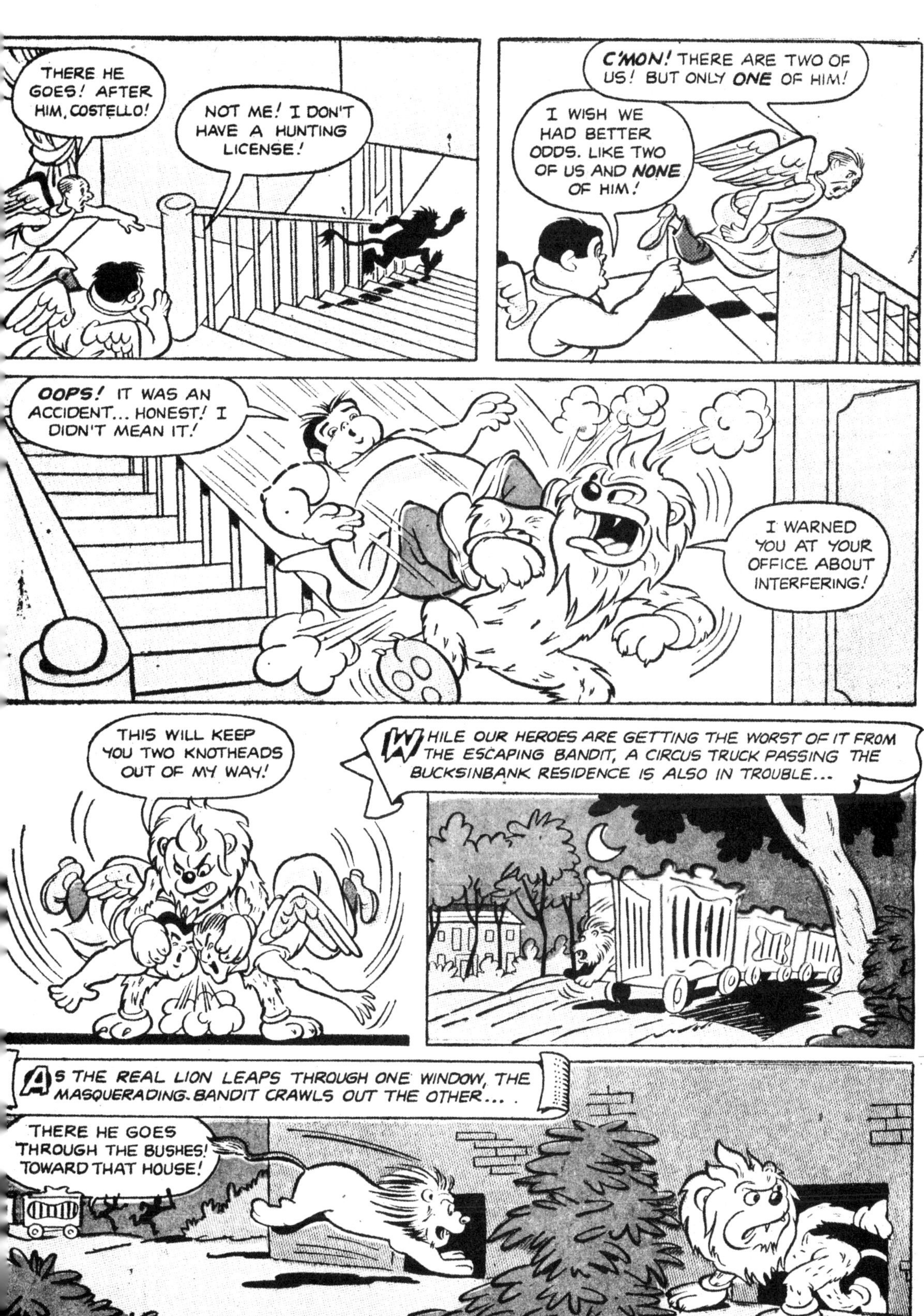
THERE HE GOES! AFTER HIM, COSTELLO!
NOT ME! I DON'T HAVE A HUNTING LICENSE!
C'MON! THERE ARE TWO OF US! BUT ONLY ONE OF HIM!
I WISH WE HAD BETTER ODDS. LIKE TWO OF US AND NONE OF HIM!
OOPS! IT WAS AN ACCIDENT... HONEST! I DIDN'T MEAN IT!
I WARNED YOU AT YOUR OFFICE ABOUT INTERFERING!
THIS WILL KEEP YOU TWO KNOTHEADS OUT OF MY WAY!
WHILE OUR HEROES ARE GETTING THE WORST OF IT FROM THE ESCAPING BANDIT, A CIRCUS TRUCK PASSING THE BUCKSINBANK RESIDENCE IS ALSO IN TROUBLE...
AS THE REAL LION LEAPS THROUGH ONE WINDOW, THE MASQUERADING BANDIT CRAWLS OUT THE OTHER...
THERE HE GOES THROUGH THE BUSHES! TOWARD THAT HOUSE!

HERE IS 'LEOPOLD!
I GOT HIM! QUICK! LET'S HAUL HIM BACK INTO THE CAGE!

MEANWHILE, INSIDE THE MANSION...
THE THIEF WENT THROUGH HERE INTO THE GAME ROOM! GET HIM!
I DON'T LIKE THIS GAME!

LOOK, COSTELLO! HE'S ASLEEP!
BE CAREFUL! MAYBE HE'S PLAY-ING POSSUM!

NO-- HE'S REALLY ASLEEP! HE MUST REALIZE THE GAME IS UP!

I'LL KEEP HIM COVERED. YOU PULL OFF HIS MASK AND WE'LL FIND OUT WHO HE IS!
HE MUST HAVE THIS MASK STUCK ON WITH CEMENT. IT WON'T COME OFF!

YOU'RE RIGHT! SNUGGEST FIT I EVER SAW!

GROWL!
HE'S JUST TRYING TO SCARE US!
AS FAR AS I'M CONCERNED, HE'S SUCCEEDED! LET'S GET OUT OF HERE!

DON'T BE SILLY, COSTELLO. THIS IS OUR BIG CHANCE! JUST TELL HIM THE JIG'S UP!
SOUNDS TO ME LIKE HE'S TELLING US OUR JIG'S UP! WATCH OUT!! HE'S COMING CLOSER!
GR-ROWL!

NOW IT'S YOUR TURN, ABBOTT! YOU STAY DOWN THERE AND TRY TO REASON WITH HIM!
AND LEAVE YOU ALONE UP THERE? NO, LOU, I'M STICKING WITH YOU THROUGH THICK AND THIN! MOVE OVER!
GR-ROWL!

A-A-ABBOTT! DO YOU NOTICE ANYTHING DIFFERENT BETWEEN THIS L-LION AND THE ONE THAT BEAT OUR HEADS TOGETHER?
YEAH. THIS ONE SEEMS TO HAVE MORE MUSCLES.

T-T-THIS ONE DOESN'T HAVE ANY H-HAIR MISSING FROM HIS M-M-MANE... MAYBE THE HAIR MRS. BUCKSINBANK GRABBED OUT GREW IN AGAIN.
Y-YOU MEAN HE'S A REAL LION!

OUCH! WE'RE FALLING ANGELS!
YOU PICK THE POOREST TIMES TO MAKE JOKES.

QUICK, COSTELLO, GET UNDER THIS SKIN! IT'S OUR ONLY CHANCE!

HEY, ABBOTT-- I THINK HE LIKES US NOW.

LET'S CRAWL AWAY AND GET HELP, WITHOUT AROUSING HIS SUSPICIONS. SAY SOMETHING NICE TO HIM, COSTELLO!
H-HELLO M-M-MATE!

LOOK! THAT'S LEOPOLD!
THEN WHO'VE WE GOT IN THE CAGE? AND WHO'S THAT MOTH-EATEN CREATURE LEOPOLD'S FOLLOWING?

YOU'RE LUCKY LEOPOLD DIDN'T GET YOU TWO JERKS MASQUERADING AS A LIONESS!
LOOK, ABBOTT! THEY'VE GOT OUR THIEF LOCKED UP IN THE CAGE!

ANYBODY KNOW THIS MAN BEHIND THE MASK?
WHY, THAT'S RALPH RUBBERNECK! MY FIANCE!
RALPH! I DON'T UNDERSTAND! YOU BOUGHT ME THE DIAMOND! WHY WOULD YOU STEAL IT?
I COULDN'T KEEP UP THE PAYMENTS, SO I HAVE TO SEND IT BACK!

NONSENSE, MY DEAR BOY! HERE'S A HUNDRED THOUSAND! PAY FOR IT OUT OF THIS!
NOW IF THAT ISN'T A SIGHT FOR A PAIR OF PRIVATE EYES!
END

ABBOTT & COSTELLO in
The BIG BRUSH-OFF!

UH... EXCUSE ME, CHUM, I JUST REMEMBERED... I GOTTA SEE SOMEONE ABOUT SOMETHING!

AM I LUCKY! COSTELLO WANDERS OFF AND LEAVE THE BLONDE FOR ME! NOW WHICH WAY DID SHE GO?

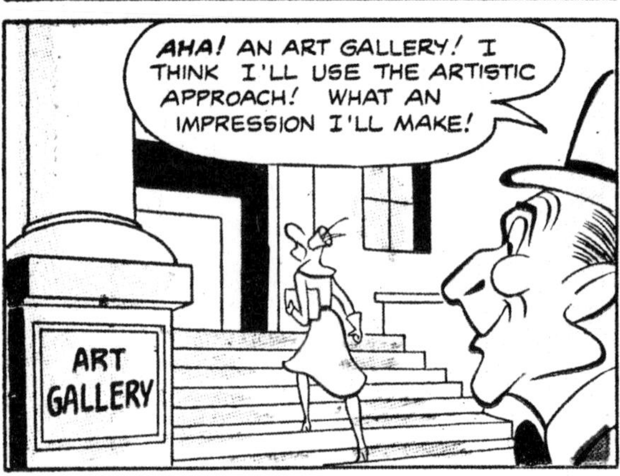
AHA! AN ART GALLERY! I THINK I'LL USE THE ARTISTIC APPROACH! WHAT AN IMPRESSION I'LL MAKE!
ART GALLERY

AS FOR COSTELLO...
POOR ABBOTT! WHAT A CHUMP! I'LL BET HE'S STILL STANDING THERE WHILE I GO AFTER THAT GEORGEOUS GIRL!

WHAT IS SHE GOING INTO THAT JOINT FOR? IF SHE WANTS TO SEE PICTURES, WHY DOESN'T SHE GO TO THE MOVIES?
ART GALLERY

WELL, HERE'S WHERE CASANOVA COSTELLO SWEEPS THAT LITTLE GAL RIGHT OFF HER FEET!
ENTRANCE TO THE ART GALLERY

YOU! YOU'RE THE MAN I'VE BEEN SEARCHING FOR!

COME CLOSER... THERE'S SOMETHING I MUST ASK YOU!
I CAN'T HELP IT... I'M IRRESISTABLE!

LATER, IN ANOTHER PART OF THE GALLERY...
AHEM! DON'T THINK I'M FRESH, MISS, BUT MY NAME IS BUD ABBOTT AND I...
HOW WONDERFUL!
PLEASE, WON'T YOU TAKE DOWN MY NAME, ADDRESS AND PHONE NUMBER?
KEEP TALKIN', SUGAR... I'M WRITING!
THAT NIGHT...
♫ SOME ENCHANTED EVENING... ♫ ♫ ♫... I'LL BE OUT MOST OF TOMORROW, LITTLE PAL!
A PENNY FOR A KISS... TUM-TI-TUM... ♫ YEAH... ME, TOO, BUD!
NEXT DAY...
COME RIGHT IN, MR. COSTELLO. SHALL WE START AT ONCE?
YOU SAID IT, HONEY-PIE! AND TO THINK THAT YESTERDAY WE WERE STRANGERS!
YOU'RE PERFECT! JUST THE TYPE I'VE BEEN LOOKING FOR! WITH YOU AS MY MODEL, I'M SURE TO WIN THE SCULPTURE CONTEST, MR. COSTELLO!
OH, JUST CALL ME LOU!!
I'LL BE AS GREAT AS MICHAELANGELO! EVEN HIS NAME MAKES ME SWOON!
WHO'S THAT-- YOUR BOYFRIEND?
SILLY BOY! BUT YOU'RE CUTE!
SHE'S CUTE TOO! I WONDER WHEN SHE'LL PROPOSE!

AND WHAT OF ROMEO ABBOTT? THE MINUTE COSTELLO LEAVES...
YOU'RE PERFECT. JUST THE TYPE I'VE BEEN LOOKING FOR. WITH YOU AS MY MODEL, I'M SURE TO WIN THE SCULPTURE CONTEST!

CELLINI! RODIN! THEY WERE REAL SCULPTORS!
OH, THEY WERE JUST A BUNCH OF **CHISELERS!** FORGET THEM! YOU'VE GOT ME!

IF ONLY MEN WERE MORE :SIGH: **ARTISTIC** NOWADAYS!
WHAT MAKES YOU THINK I'M NOT?

THAT NIGHT...
HOW DO I LOOK IN THIS POSE, ABBOTT... HANDSOME?
COSTELLO, CAN'T YOU STOP THIS HORSEPLAY? LET'S TALK ABOUT SOMETHING SERIOUS LIKE **ART!**

BUT THAT WAS ARTISTIC! DON'T YOU KNOW THE **REAL** ME! I'M CRAZY ABOUT ART!
THAT'S FUNNY... SO AM **I!**

Y'KNOW, PAL-O'-MINE... I'VE BEEN **THINKING...**
THAT'S FUNNY... SO HAVE **I!**

ABBOTT, LET'S FORGET THIS SORDID, CHEAP ATMOSPHERE AND BETAKE OURSELVES TO A HIGHER SPHERE!
LIKE FER INSTANCE, GREENWICH VILLAGE!

AND SO...
WE HAVE BEEN LIVING TOO FAR AWAY FROM THE FINER THINGS OF LIFE!
YEAH! WE'LL FIND A NICE, CULTURED ATTIC DOWNTOWN AND LIVE LIKE **ARTISTS!**

THE NEXT DAY, COSTELLO RETURNS TO HIS VOLUNTARY JOB OF POSING...
MR. COSTELLO, I'VE GREAT NEWS FOR YOU!
YOU GONNA PROPOSE MARRIAGE?
THE ART GALLERY IS RUNNING A PAINTING CON-TEST, TOO!
ENTER ME! ENROLL ME! GIMME A BRUSH... GIMME PAINT! I'LL WIN THAT CONTEST FOR YOU!!
WHILE UNKNOWN TO COSTELLO...
SELL ME BRUSHES! PAINTS! I'VE GOT
SELL ME TO WIN A CONTEST!
ARTISTS' MATERIALS
IN SECRET...
THAT'S WHAT I CALL PAINTING! NOT EVEN AN EIGHT-YEAR OLD COULD DO BETTER!
AND UNKNOWN TO ABBOTT...
WITH MY TALENT, I CAN'T LOSE! BUT I'D BETTER HIDE THIS STUFF SO ABBOTT CAN'T FIND IT!
OH, HELLO, COSTELLO! I WAS JUST--GOING OUT FOR A WALK!
GREAT! SWELL! HURRY BACK!
THE MINUTE ABBOTT'S BACK IS TURNED...
WHY SHOULD I FIGHT IT? I'M A GENIUS! I COULDN'T DO BETTER WITH MY EYES OPEN!
HEY, I'M MIXED UP! IS THIS MY PAINTING OR THE RAG I USED TO CLEAN MY BRUSHES ON?

...AND AT NIGHT...
NOW THAT COSTELLO IS ASLEEP, I CAN WORK!
ZZZZZZZZZZZ ZZZZZZ

MY THINGS ARE HIDDEN WHERE HE'LL NEVER FIND THEM-- IN HIS OWN CLOSET!!

OUCH! IT'S AN AVALANCHE!
ZZZZZZ ZZZZZ

WHAT'S THIS? IT CAN'T BE! BUT IT IS!

SO! COSTELLO'S BEEN PAINTING BEHIND MY BACK! HE'S BEEN TRYING TO WIN THE CONTEST! MAYBE HE'S EVEN AFTER MY GIRL! THE SNEAK!

SAY-- HE'S GOOD! OR AM I HOLDING IT UPSIDE DOWN? THIS MUST BE HIS PAINTING... OR IS IT THE RAG HE USES TO CLEAN HIS BRUSHES ON? HMMM...

ALL'S FAIR IN LOVE AND ART, EVEN WHEN IT'S UNFAIR! I'LL SEND HIS RAG TO THE GALLERY!
FROM: L. COSTELLO
TO: DOWNTOWN ART GALLERY
123 GREENWICH ST.
NEW YORK CITY

THE MORNING OF THE CONTEST...
ER... SO LONG, ABBOTT, OLD PAL! I'M GOIN' THIS WAY!
SO LONG, COSTELLO, OLD CHUM. I'M GOING THAT WAY!

INSIDE THE GALLERY...
LATELY, ABBOTT HAS BECOME VERY UNCOUTH... A LOW-BROW! WHY DO I BOTHER WITH SUCH RIFF-RAFF...
SMACK

ABBOTT!! WHAT ARE YOU DOING HERE?
I HAPPEN TO BE AN ARTIST WITH AN ENTRY IN THE CONTEST!

THAT'S A LIE! I'M AN ARTIST! AND I'M WINNING THE CONTEST!
OH, YOU KNOW EACH OTHER! ISN'T THAT SWEET!

WHEN I WIN THE CONTEST, WILL YOU BE MINE?
DON'T BE FOOLISH! SHE'S GONNA BE MINE!

STOP WASTING TIME AND HURRY! THEY'RE ANNOUNCING THE WINNER!!

TO LEONARDO COSTELLO FOR HIS UNUSUAL CREATION!
AWK!
HEY! THAT'S NOT MY PAINTING! IT'S THE RAG I USE TO CLEAN MY BRUSHES...

YOU'RE WONDERFUL! I MUST KISS YOU!
HMM... MAYBE IT IS MY PAINTING AFTER ALL!

COSTELLO, YOU BACK-STABBER, YOU'VE **RUINED** MY ART CAREER AND **STOLEN** THE ONLY GIRL I EVER LOVED... **BAA-A-A!!**
DON'T WORRY, ABBOTT, I FORGIVE YOU!

YOU FORGIVE **ME?** SO HELP ME, I'LL...
ABBOTT, CONTROL YOURSELF! THINK OF MY TALENT!
C'MON, THEY'RE ANNOUNCING THE **SCULPTURE PRIZE!**

THIS MAGNIFICENT WORK ENTITLED "TOOTH-PICK AND ORANGE," PERFECT IN DESIGN AND BALANCE--
YOU BOYS WILL BE **ESPECIALLY** PROUD OF THIS, BECAUSE THANKS TO YOU... **I'VE WON!**
HEY, ABBOTT!! DID YOU POSE FOR HER, TOO? IS **THAT** SUPPOSED TO BE US?

I'M AN ORANGE, EH?
SO... I'M A TOOTHPICK, EH?

YOU **WONDERFUL** DARLINGS! I'M GOING TO KISS YOU **BOTH!** YOU WERE **DIVINE MODELS!**
WOMAN, STAND OFF!

YOU INSULTED MY FRIEND ORANGE... I MEAN, COSTELLO! I TAKE BACK MY PROPOSAL OF MARRIAGE!
ME, TOO! TO THINK YOU NEARLY BUSTED UP A BEAUTIFUL FRIENDSHIP! C'MON, TOOTHPICK ... I MEAN ABBOTT!

AS I WAS SAYING, CHUM, NO DAME WILL EVER COME BETWEEN US AGAIN! UNITED WE STAND... DIVIDED WE... HMM... SEE YOU LATER, TOOTHPICK!
COSTELLO, **COME BACK!** OH BROTHER... THIS IS **THE END!**

ABBOTT and COSTELLO in Water, Water, Everywhere...

ABBOTT, THIS DIVINING ROD IS WONDERFUL! IT ALWAYS POINTS TO WATER!

LOOK AT US NOW-- STANDING IN THE RAIN, PUSHING A TRUCK!
NO EXCITEMENT IN OUR LIVES ANY MORE!

WHA-- OHHH!
ABBOTT!!

HEY, YOU'RE RUINING MY CHANCES FOR SURVIVAL. THESE SUSPENDERS AREN'T STRONG ENOUGH FOR TWO!
SHUT UP AND LET ME THINK!

IF I CAN HOOK MY BELT TO THAT ROCK, WE'LL HAVE SOMETHING MORE CONCRETE TO HOLD ON TO...

...THEN WE CAN CLIMB THIS CLIFF! HEY--WHERE'D THE BIG DRAFT COME FROM?

BOY! LOOK DOWN THERE! WERE WE EVER LUCKY!
BR-R-R! LET'S FIND SHELTER. I'M C-C-COLD!

THREE MILES DOWN THE ROAD...
LOOK, ABBOTT! A HOUSE!

IT'S DESERTED!
WELL, WE'LL UN-DESERT IT!
THIS HOUSE IS 100 % HAUNTED!!

UMM... SOME COFFEE, BUT NO WATER!
MUST BE SOME IN THE KITCHEN!
COFFEE

THE TAP IS DRY!
MY DIVINING ROD WILL COME IN HANDY! LUCKY I DIDN'T LOSE MY PANTS!

HALF AN HOUR LATER...
I'VE BEEN DIGGING AND DIGGING AND NO WATER YET!

THE DIVINER IS POINTING UP NOW INSTEAD OF DOWN!

THAT CAN MEAN ONLY ONE THING!
YEAH! THAT YOUR WATER DIVINER'S A PHONEY!

RAIN! YOU SEE, ABBOTT, IT KNEW THERE WAS WATER UP THERE!
EVEN THE WEATHER MAN COULD TELL THAT KNUCKLE-HEAD!

I'VE ALMOST CAUGHT ENOUGH TO MAKE SOME COFFEE!
A-ABBOTT! THERE'S A BILL ON THIS CAN AND IT'S DATED YESTERDAY!

THEN SOMEBODY MUST'VE BEEN HERE!
AND THAT SOMEBODY MIGHT STILL BE HERE!
COFFE

STOP SHIVERING, COSTELLO, AND GET YOUR CLAMMY HANDS OFF MY SHOULDER!
WHO'S KIDDING WHO? THAT'S NOT MY HAND!

BOO!
A GHOST!
A TATTLE TALE GRAY GHOST!

BOO!
RUN, COSTELLO, RUN!!

D-DON'T LET HIM IN, ABBOTT! I'M S-SCARED OF G-GHOSTS!
PILE SOME FURNITURE IN FRONT OF THE DOOR!

EXPECTING SOMEBODY?

THAT NIGHT, ABBOTT AND COSTELLO SIT IT OUT IN THE COUNTY JAIL! FOR DISCOVERING OIL? WELL, NOT QUITE...

ABBOTT and COSTELLO

Two Knights in a Daze

HELP! PUT ME DOWN!

THROUGH THE DESERTED STREETS IN THE WEE HOURS BEFORE DAWN, MOVES A SINISTER FIGURE... A THIN MAN, CARRYING OVER HIS SHOULDER A HULKING BODY! SOME MURDERER AND HIS HAPLESS VICTIM?

YOU'LL NEVER ESCAPE ME... NEVER!

OF ALL THE SKINNY, RICKETY, SWAY-BACKED, SAD-EYED, BONE-HEADED ANIMALS... NOT, YOU, COS-TELLO! I MEAN THE HORSE!
I KINDA LIKE HIM! SO LONG... YAWN... BUDDY, WISH ME LUCK! GEE-YUP.. YAWN... GEE-YUP...
HARD WORK NEVER HURT ANYBODY... ESPECIALLY COSTELLO!
ZZZZZZZZ!
HEY, ABBOTT, HOW DID YOU GET HERE?
THIS IS A DREAM, AIN'T IT? ANYTHING CAN HAPPEN IN A DREAM!
ANYTHING IS HAPPENING!
ABBOTT, LOOK AT THAT HORSE! HE'S PRETTIER THAN SEA BISCUIT!
PALLY! THEM'S DE FOIST KIND WOIDS ME EARS HAVE HOID IN NINE HUNDRED YEARS!
Y'SEE, PALLY... ME, HOIMAN, I'M ENCHANTED! I BEEN UNDER DIS SPELL EVER SINCE KNIGHTHOOD WUZ IN FLOWER. Y'KNOW... KING ARTHUR AN' ALL DAT STUFF!
KNIGHTS! FLOWERS! PHOOEY! LISTEN... I WASN'T BORN YESTERDAY EITHER! I NEVER MET A HORSE YET WHO WASN'T A LIAR!
SAY, CHUM, WHO'S YOUR WISE-CRACKIN' FRIEND? I'LL SHOW HIM WHO'S A LIAR!
FOLLOW ME, MEN!
C...CAN WE H... HELP IT?
MILK

OOOH, I CAN'T LOOK!
DON'T BE SCARED, PALLY! WE'RE IN ME OWN HOME TERRITORY!
WHEN KNIGHTHOOD WAS IN FLOWER...
HEAR YE! HEAR YE! BE IT KNOWN THAT THE WINNER OF THIS TOURNEY WILL BE AWARDED THE FIRST PRIZE OF RESCUING THE PRINCESS HILDA FROM THE AWFUL DRAGON!
FORSOOTH! WHO WANTS TO RESCUE HER?
WHAT'S THE MATTER WITH THAT BIG TIN-CAN? AIN'T HE ROMANTIC?
TO ARMS, KNIGHTS! THE CONTEST BEGINS!
BOINGG! BULL'S-EYE! YOU MEN NOIVOUS OR SOMETHIN'?
YES... THE VERY THOUGHT OF PRINCESS HILDA MAKES US SHUDDER!
I SURRENDER TO YOUR SUPERIOR POWERS!
THIS BOY MUST HAVE HEARD OF ME SOMEPLACE!
HEY, STAND UP AN' FIGHT!
YOU, NOBLE STRANGER, ARE THE VICTOR! OUR PRAYERS HAVE BEEN ANSWERED... WE LOSE!
HE WINS! ALL HAIL, ALL-CONQUERING RESCUER OF OUR... UGH!... PRINCESS HILDA!
THAT'S ME ALL RIGHT!
THREE TESTS AWAIT YOU, FEARLESS ONE! THE FOREST OF EVIL... THE ICE MOUNTAIN... AND THEN---THE AWFUL DRAGON! IF YOU OVERCOME THESE, YOU WILL WIN THE PRINCESS HILDA!
YOU HAD TO GET US INTO THIS, YOU, YOU... HORSE!
LEAVE HERMAN ALONE, ABBOTT! HE'S GOTTA LEAD US TO... THE FOREST OF EVIL!

DARK AND GLOOMY IS THE FOREST... THE HORRID DOMAIN OF THE WICKED WITCH!
IT'S ALL THAT NAG'S FAULT! IF I EVER SAW A PHONY---
HEH-HEH-HEH... VICTIMS! AND JUST IN TIME FOR DINNER! I THINK I'LL PUT THEM IN DEEP FREEZE!
FAT ONE, THIN ONE, WITCH'S PREY... FREEZE... WITHIN YOUR TRACKS, I SAY!
CAPTURED BY THE WICKED WITCH!
WOULD YOU...HEH-HEH...STEP IN HERE, MY BOY? DON'T WANT TO BE LATE FOR DINNER, YOU KNOW! (CACKLE-CACKLE!)
NOTHING WE LIKE BETTER THAN DINNER! AND A BATH FIRST! ISN'T SHE A DOLL?
A CUP OF COFFEE... A SANDWICH... AND YOU-OOO...
AND YOU-OOO! LOOK, COSTELLO, WE AREN'T GOING TO EAT... WE'RE GONNA BE EATEN... COOKED!
TALKING ABOUT COOKING, I KNEW THERE WAS SOMETHING I WANTED TO ASK YOU, WITCHIE... WHAT'S A GOOD RECIPE FOR BOILED BEEF?
BOILED BEEF... HEH-HEH! I ALWAYS TRY TO GET A PIECE OF FAT, JUICY, TENDER BEEF... HEH-HEH!
BUT WHY WASTE TIME TALKING... ARE YOU FEELING WELL DONE YET?
SUPPOSE YOU GET A SCRAWNY, SKINNY, STRINGY SIDE OF BEEF? DO YOU ADD A PINCH OF SOMETHING?
EEEEEK! YOU PINCHED ME!
REAL HEP, AIN'T SHE? ALL RIGHT, WITCHIE... STEW IN YOUR OWN JUICE!

WELL, I SURE DUSTED HER OFF! WHAT'S THE NEXT PERIL, HERMAN?
I T'INK WE GOTTA CLIMB UP DA ICE MOUNTAIN UPON WHICH DA PRINCESS IS IMPRISONED!
ICE MOUNTAIN! STEEP, SLITHERY AND SLIPPERY! TERRIBLY TREACHEROUS! IMPERVIOUS! IMPREGNABLE! CAN OUR HEROES CONQUER IT??
DAT'S DE DRAGON'S CASTLE UP DERE... PRINCESS HILDA'S HIDEOUT!
WELL, WE'VE SEEN IT! NOW LET'S BEAT IT!
NEVER! FOLLOW ME, VARLET! ONWARD AND... UPWARD!
HMMM... ICY, AIN'T IT?
WELL, SIR HOLE-IN-THE-HEAD... WHAT DO WE DO NOW?
GROAN... HELP ME UP, SQUIRE! I'M GONNA MAKE A MOLEHILL OUT OF THIS MOUNTAIN!
THIS REMINDS ME OF THE TIME MY MOTHER FORGOT TO DEFROST THE REFRIGERATOR! DID MY OLD MAN SIZZLE!
WELL, THAT WAS FAST! I KNEW THIS THING WAS GOOD FOR SOMETHING... I NEVER COULD LIGHT CIGARETTES WITH IT!
DON'T LOOK NOW, HERO... BUT-- WE GOT... ER... ANOTHER VISITOR!

THE AWFUL DRAGON!
LET'S USE STRATEGY! RETREAT!
NEVER! FOLLOW ME, PEASANT! CHARGE!
AW, WHO'S AFRAID OF THE BIG, BAD DRAGON!
I AM! AND WHO'S FOLLOWING WHO? STOP SHOVING!
COSTELLO, IT'S HORRIBLE! HE'S BREATHING SMOKE AND FIRE AT US!
YEAH...REMINDS ME OF THE TIME MY MOTHER LEFT THE STOVE LIT! WAS MY OLD MAN SORE!
NOW'S YOUR CHANCE, ABBOTT! HIT'M! GIVE'M THE OLD RABBIT PUNCH!
I GIVE UP...I GIVE UP.. I GIVE UP...
???
HEH! WE SCARED HIM TO DEATH!
WE DIDN'T SCARE HIM... SHE DID! THAT BATTLEAXE IS THE PRINCESS HILDA!
PLEASE, SIR DRAGON, WE APOLOGIZE! TAKE HER BACK! I'LL THROW IN A BONUS FOR YOU! KEEP HER!
WE MADE A MISTAKE! WE GOT THE WRONG PARTY! TAKE HER BACK!
I DON'T WANT HER, YOU CAN HAVE HER, SHE'S TOO TOUGH FOR ME!
HMMM... A FINE PAIR OF SPECIMENS THEY SENT! COME HERE, YOU!
!!!!

AND SO... ALL HAIL THE CONQUERING HEROES!
AS A REWARD, ONE OF THESE GLORIOUS KNIGHTS WINS... THE HAND OF PRINCESS HILDA!
WHAT A HORRIBLE IDEA!
NYAAA! OLD BAG!
BUT... WHICH ONE?
LOOK INTO MY EYES, FAT ONE! YOU'RE CUTE!
NOW YOU! YOU'RE REPULSIVE, BUT I LIKE THAT DESPERATE LOOK IN YOUR EYES!
OOCHY-KOOCHY, I CHOOSE YOU!
NO! HELP ME, SOMEBODY! COSTELLO... HERMAN... PAL!
WHO, ME? I'M A PHONY... REMEMBER?
DID I SAY THAT? I MUST HAVE BEEN OUT OF MY MIND! YOU'RE SMART, HONEST, HANDSOME...
I CAN'T RESIST FLATTERY! ALL RIGHT, PALLY, GET OFF'N YOUR KNEES.
ZZZ... MUCH ROUGHER FLIGHT THIS TIME... SNORZZZ...
COSTELLO! BABIES ALL OVER TOWN ARE CRYING FOR THEIR MILK! WAKE UP!
SNORZZ... ZZZ... MUCH ROUGHER FLIGHT THIS TIME... HUH? HEEEY, ABBOTT, THIS CAN'T BE!
WHAT'S THE IDEA OF YOU AND THAT NAG FALLIN' ASLEEP!
ASLEEP! WAS IT ALL... A DREAM? HERMAN, TELL ME THE TRUTH! SPEAK TO ME!
NEIGHHHH!

Abbott and Costello DISCOVER AMERICA

Man the mains'l! Reef the tops'l! Brace yourselves! These two old salts are about to hit the deck!

COSTELLO, I FEEL LIKE A FOOL IN THIS OUTFIT! AFTER ALL, WE'RE ONLY TAKING A FERRY TO PATTERSON, NEW JERSEY!

STOW THAT BILGE, ABBOTT! A SEA VOYAGE IS A SEA VOYAGE!

ALL ABOARD FOR LIVERPOOL...
SAY, ABBOTT, Y' KNOW... THIS DON'T LOOK LIKE THE WEEHAWKEN FERRY!
LOOK, PERKINS, A COMMODORE!
ACCORDING TO THE ADMIRALTY CODE, I MUST SURRENDER COMMAND OF MY VESSEL TO HIM!

IN ACCORDANCE WITH REGULATION 23, T. M. XXX, P.S. 49A -- THIS VESSEL, SIR, IS YOURS IN THE NAME OF HIS MAJESTY, THE KING!
HONEST? WELL, THANKS! I REALLY DON'T DESERVE IT!

COSTELLO, ARE YOU CRAZY? THE PASSENGERS ON THIS SHIP EXPECT TO LAND IN ENGLAND!
AT EASE, SEAMAN ABBOTT! I KNOW WHAT I'M DOING!

♫ ANCHORS AWEIGH, MY BOYS, ANCHORS AWEIGH... ♫ TWO POINTS TO LARBOARD... ONE POINT TO STARBOARD...
MAYBE HE DOES KNOW WHAT HE'S DOING AND I'M CRAZY!

AND, UNDER THE POWERFUL HANDS OF THE BRILLIANT NAVIGATOR...
WELL, ABBOTT, WHAT DO YOU SAY NOW? THERE'S ENGLAND! LAND HO!
YESSIR -- AAH, SHADDUP! BRR... I'M FREEZING! YOU... BRRR... STEERED US TO THE NORTH POLE!

THE NORTH POLE? HMM.. I MUST'VE HAD AN OLD ROAD MAP!
I COULD.... BRR... KILL HIM NOW AND PLEAD TEMPORARY INSANITY.

WHILE, FROM A NEARBY ICE FLOE...
GET THAT, PERCY! ANOTHER SUNDAY DRIVER LOST!
AND PIPE THAT HUNK OF BLUBBER ON THE BRIDGE!

YOU... YOU HUNK OF BLUBBER! NOW SEE WHAT YOU'VE GOTTEN US INTO!
NEVER MIND, SAILOR! WHAT I'VE DONE ONCE, I CAN DO AGAIN. STAND BACK!
MAN THE MAINS'L... TOP THE TOPS'L... PRESS THAT CLUTCH... GIVE 'ER GAS! TOTE THAT BARGE! LIFT THAT BALE! AND FULL STEAM AHEAD!
AYE, AYE, SIR... AYE, AYE, SIR!
I FEEL SICK!

GOT TO REMEMBER TO PUT MY HAND OUT ON THIS LEFT TURN! THAT'LL TAKE US TO ENGLAND!
COSTELLO, CAN'T YOU STOP ZIGGING AND ZAG A LITTLE?

AND SO, WE TAKE OUR LEAVE OF THE GENTLE ARTIC AND, IN THE COURSE OF TIME... DARKEST AFRICA!"
COSTELLO, YOU'VE STEERED US WRONG AGAIN!
MMM... WHO CARES? WHILE WE'RE HERE, WE MIGHT AS WELL BE FRIENDLY!

LOOK, BEAUTIFUL DOLLS -- LOUIE IS HERE! ALOHA! ALOHA! STICK WITH ME, ABBOTT-- HEY! THAT AIN'T FRIENDLY!

HERE WE GO AGAIN!

TO ARMS, MEN! BATTLE STATIONS!
NO, YOU DON'T! YOU'VE GONE FAR ENOUGH, COSTELLO! THIS TIME WE'RE GOING TO LIVERPOOL!

I WARN YOU, COSTELLO, TURN THIS SHIP OVER TO THE RIGHTFUL CAPTAIN OR I'LL--
SAILOR, I AM THE RIGHTFUL CAPTAIN! WHERE'S THE DASHBOARD? WHERE'S THE STEERING WHEEL? I'M TAKING OVER PERSONALLY!!

GET AWAY FROM THAT WHEEL! TAKE... YOUR... HANDS... OFF... THAT... WHEEL!
SEAMAN ABBOTT, THIS IS INSUBORDINATION! YOU'RE ATTACKING THE PERSON OF AN ADMIRAL!

AN ADMIRAL? WHEN DID YOU GET PROMOTED?
I PROMOTED MYSELF FOR MY GOOD WORK! FOR THE LAST TIME, LET ME LOOSE!
BANG!
AMERICA
ENG.
AUS.

HEY, ABBOTT, WHAT'S THIS... SMOKE?...FIRE? ABANDON SHIP! THE CAPTAIN GOES DOWN WITH HIS SHIP! WHERE'S THE CAPTAIN?
AAH, PINHEAD! IT'S ONLY FOG!... WHAT YOU'RE ALWAYS IN!

AND WHEN THE FOG CLEARS...
LAND! LAND AHEAD!
LAND, EH? ABOUT TIME! MAYBE I OUGHTA PROMOTE MYSELF AGAIN! WHAT'S HIGHER THAN ADMIRAL?

SEE, SEAMAN ABBOTT, I TOLD YOU WE'D MAKE ENGLAND... ER... LIVERPOOL... ER... WHAT'S THAT?

THAT, ADMIRAL COSTELLO, HAPPENS TO BE THE STATUE OF LIBERTY... IN NEW YORK!
I THOUGHT SHE LOOKED FAMILIAR
I KNEW A DAME LOOKED JUST LIKE HER IN PASSAIC!

NOW THEY'LL HAVE THE COPS OUT AFTER YOU... AND THE NAVY... THE G-MEN...AND THE MARINES! THEN THERE'S THE SOUTH AFRICAN WELFARE COMMISSION AND THE SOCIETY FOR THE PREVENTION OF CRUELTY TO ESKIMOES ... AND HERE THEY COME!
THERE HE IS-- THE LITTLE TUBBY ONE!

GRAB HIM! SWING HIM UP! DON'T LET HIM GET AWAY!
THIS IS THE GUY... THE SHORT, FAT ONE!
LISTEN YOU-- I'M NO SHORTER OR FATTER THAN ANY MAN MY SIZE!
I WARNED YOU! THEY'LL COURTMARTIAL YOU-- STRING YOU UP!

IN HONOR OF THE COMMODORE'S BRILLIANT NAVIGATION, HIS BRAVERY IN THE FACE OF MENACE, HIS FORTITUDE IN BRINGING US SAFELY THROUGH UNSEEN DANGERS...
THAT'S ME, ALL RIGHT!

BEFORE GOING ASHORE FOR THE CELEBRATION IN YOUR HONOR, SIR, WOULD YOU LIKE TO GIVE ONE LAST ORDER AS COMMANDER OF THIS SHIP?
YEP, SURE! I THINK THE SHIP DESERVES IT.

CLAP THAT SAILOR INTO THE BRIG!
ISN'T THERE ANY JUSTICE LEFT?

AND WHEN THE FOG CLEARS...
ONE TICKET TO PATTERSON, NEW JERSEY, PLEASE!
QUEEN MARY

ABBOTT & COSTELLO in OUT IN THE BAA-AA-AAD LAND!

NO, NO, COSTELLO! THIS IS THE HORSE!

WE'LL GO TO THE DOWDY-DUDY RANCH! YOU WILL SWEEP THIS... UGH... SWEET GIRL OFF HER FEET WITH YOUR COWBOY SKILL, YOUR DARING, FRANKNESS, MANLINESS! AND THEN... YOU WILL MARRY HER!
BRACK! WHISH ONE ISZH THE HORSZH!

WE'LL BE IN CLOVER! THINK OF ALL THE LARD AND FAT YOU'LL OWN!
NO! NO! NO!! NO! NO! NO! NO!

WE'LL TAKE TWENTY GALLONS WORTH OF THOSE TEN-GALLON HATS!
HATS
NO!
A COUPLE OF PAIRS OF BOW-LEGGED PANTS!
SUITS
NO!
AND A SHOTGUN, A SIX-GUN AND A WINCHESTER RIFLE FOR MY PAL... KILLER COSTELLO!
NO!

TWENTY HOURS LATER...
I TOLD YOU A THOUSAND TIMES ABBOTT... I'M NOT GOING!
I HAVE A SURPRISE FOR YOU, COSTELLO-BOY... WE'RE HERE!

HEY, ABBOTT, GET A LOAD OF THAT OLD COYOTE!
SHAME ON YOU, COSTELLO... YOU ARE SPEAKING OF THE WOMAN YOU LOVE!
Dude Ranch

ABBOTT, LEMME GO! EAST IS EAST AND WEST IS WEST AND THE WRONG ONE I HAVE CHOSE!
DON'T TRY TUH MAKE A BREAK FER IT, HOMBRE ...I'M DESPERATE!

SO-O-O... UNDER ABBOTT'S WATCHFUL EYE... LASSOIN' LOU SETTLES DOWN TO ROMANCE ON THE RANGE...
HEY, ABBOTT, EXPLAIN TO THIS COW THAT I GOT'M LICKED! OWCH!
TENDERFOOT! YOU'LL NEVER IMPRESS CECILY THAT WAY!

LET ME SHOW YUH HOW IT'S DONE, PARD!
OWCH!
THAT COWBOY WITH THE LASSO IS SO MANLY! OOH, I LIKE HIM!

AND...
DARK IN HERE, AIN'T IT, ABBOTT? HOW DO I GET THIS THING STARTED?
OMIGOSH, YOU'LL KILL YOURSELF! DROP THAT GUN, LOUIE!

WATCH ME! CRAK! CRAK! CRAK!
SO WILD! SO WESTERN! OOOH, I ADORE HIM!

THEN...
ABBOTT, THERE AIN'T NO STEERING WHEEL ON THIS THING! AND WHERE'S THE BRAKES??
COSTELLO! WAIT! GET OFF BEFORE HE GETS THE IDEA YOU'RE AFRAID OF HIM!

PAY ATTENTION! SHOW'M WHO'S BOSS! SEE? GIT MOVIN' HOSS!
HE'S JUST SWEEPIN' ME OFF MY FEET!

HOW'M I DOIN' ABBOTT? WHAT'S NEXT ON THE PROGRAM?
I THINK YOU'VE IMPRESSED HER ENOUGH! IT'S TIME TO PROPOSE!

ABBOTT... PLEASE... BUDDY... CAN'T WE WAIT A LITTLE WHILE? ABOUT A HUNDRED YEARS OR SO?
COSTELLO, THE TIME IS RIPE! YOU ARE GOING TO PROPOSE... NOW!

MAKE IT ROMANTIC, POETIC ...SOMETHING LIKE... "CECILY SIMPKINS, QUEEN OF FAT AND LARD, WON'T YOU BE AN EVER-LOVIN' PARD???
???
???

OH, HOW I'VE BEEN WAITING... YEARNING... FOR THIS MOMENT! YES, YES, A THOUSAND TIMES YES! MY DARLING... DARLING... ABBOTT!

LET'S SEE, HOW DOES THAT GO AGAIN? "WON'T YOU BE MY EVER-LOVIN'..."
LOVER! WE'LL BE MARRIED AT ONCE!
OMIGOSH! IT'S A CASE OF MISTAKEN IDENTITY!

BEFORE BUD ABBOTT CAN SAY, "I'M TOO YOUNG TO GET MARRIED..."
WE'LL WANT A REAL WESTERN WEDDING, JUDGE... WON'T WE, DARLING?
TRAPPED! I CAN'T STAND IT... GOTTA ESCAPE---

ISN'T HE CUTE? HE'S STARTING TO ACT LIKE A HUSBAND ALREADY!
I DIDN'T FIGURE ABBOTT WAS SO EAGER!

IF I CAN ONLY GET A COUPLE OF MILES HEAD START...
OOOF!
ABBOTT, COME BACK! I FORGOT SOMETHING!

I FORGOT TO CONGRATULATE YOU! I HOPE YOU'LL BE VERY HAPPY!
I AM SHAKING WITH F-F-FRIGHT! Y-YOU BACHELOR!

IT'S TIME FOR THE WEDDING, AND THE WEDDING PARTY'S GALLOPED OFF, BUT...
BET I KNOCKED 'EM DEAD IN THIS FULL DRESS SUIT... HEY! WHERE IS EVERYBODY? GOTTA HURRY... THEY CAN'T START THE CEREMONY WITHOUT THE BEST MAN!

H---HELLO, HORSIE... YOU MUST BE WAITING FOR ME! DID-DID MY PAL ABBOTT TELL YOU ABOUT ME? I PREFER A NICE, SMOOTH RIDE... NO MORE THAN FIFTEEN MILES AN HOUR...

ALL CLEAR? OKAY, ON TO THE WEDDING... GIDDAP! HEY! WHERE AM I? THIS HORSE HAS NO HEAD! IT'S A HEADLESS HORSE!

NOW WE'RE GETTING SOMEWHERE... BUT WHERE?
THUD!

WOULD YOU PLEASE LET ME KNOW WHEN WE GET TO THE WEDDING? I'D LIKE TO GET OFF THERE, IF YOU DON'T MIND?
AS THE SUN SINKS LOW IN THE WESTERN SKY, A LONE HORSEMAN RIDES BRAVELY ACROSS THE PRAIRIE, THROUGH THE GULCH... INTO THE CANYON ... OVER THE RAVINE... ALONG THE MESA...

AND, LIKE A STREAK OF PRAIRIE LIGHTNIN'... STRAIGHT INTO THE WEDDING PARLOR!
WHOA! ALL ASHORE! DROP THE ANCHOR! LAST STOP! CEASE! HOW DO I TURN THIS THING OFF? H-E-E-E-EY ABBOTT, STOP 'M!
NOTHING CAN HELP ME NOW! I DO... I DO... I DO... I DO... I DO!

I'M SO NERVOUS! DO I KNOW WHAT I'M DOING? I MUST BE OUTA MY MIND!
I FEEL FAINT... OOOH...
BUMP!

NO 'UN SHOOTS UP SAD SAM STUBBS AN' LIVES! YUH VARMINT... I'LL PLUG YUH DAID
BANG!
BANG!

GEE, ABBOTT, I THINK HE'S MAD!
COSTELLO, OLD FRIEND, OLD PAL, OLD LIFE SAVER! WAIT FOR ME!

ABBOTT, I DON'T KNOW HOW TO SAY THIS, BUT...I'M SORRY! I'LL NEVER FORGIVE MYSELF FOR BREAKING UP YOUR WEDDING! LET'S TURN THE HORSE AROUND AND HEAD BACK TO CECILY!
YOU AND YOUR CRAZY IDEAS! SHUT UP AND KEEP RIDING!

ABBOTT AND COSTELLO in

TAKEN for a RIDE!

UNDER CONSTRUCTION
PROCEED AT YOUR OWN RISK!

HURRY UP, COSTELLO! WE'RE AT THE STATION!
O.K. ABBOTT! I'M PRACTICALLY OFF. DUM-DE-DUM. I'M AN OLD SMOOTHIE!

GOODBYE, SIR PUDDING HEAD!
GRUMPH! WHY, YOU UPSTART!

HEY! THAT'S YOUR FRIEND FROM THE WASHROOM. WHAT'S HE SO SORE ABOUT?
I DUNNO, ABBOTT! TSK-TSK! SHOULD WE STOP AND TRY TO PATCH THINGS UP?

NO, RUN! IF HE GETS US WITH THAT RAZOR, WE'LL HAVE TO BE PATCHED UP!

WHEW! WE GAVE HIM THE SLIP. WONDER WHO HE IS?
I DON'T KNOW, BUT HE'D MAKE A GOOD BUTCHER, THE WAY HE SLINGS THAT RAZOR!

BOY! IT SURE FEELS GOOD TO BE AWAY FROM THE ARMY. AWAY FROM THE LOW BRASS, THE MEDIUM BRASS AND THE HIGH BRASS!
FOR ONCE YOU ECHO MY SENTIMENTS EXACTLY!

COSTELLO! WHERE DID YOU GET THAT JACKET?
OH, PARDON ME, GENERAL. I DIDN'T SEE YOU STANDING THERE!
KNUCKLE-BRAIN! THAT'S A MIRROR YOU'RE SALUTING!
PARKING

I REPEAT! WHERE DID YOU GET THAT JACKET?
I DON'T KNOW. YOU THINK WASHINGTON HAS PROMOTED ME AND WANTED IT TO BE A SURPRISE?

I MOST CERTAINLY DO NOT! LOOK! YOU MUST HAVE TAKEN HIS JACKET BY MISTAKE!

YOU MEAN THIS PROMOTION ISN'T PERMANENT? THIS IS THE END OF ME AS A GENERAL?
IF HE EVER CATCHES YOU, IT'LL BE THE END OF YOU AS ANYTHING! AND PROBABLY THE END OF OUR FURLOUGHS, TOO!

SOMEHOW, WE HAVE TO FIGURE A WAY OF GETTING OUT OF HERE!
BUT HOW? HE'LL BE SURE TO SEE US. AFTER ALL, WE GENERALS ATTRACT A LOT OF ATTENTION.
PARKING

MEANWHILE... INSIDE THE CAR THAT ABBOTT AND COSTELLO ARE HIDING UNDER...
ZAT MUST BE ZEE GENERAL AGENT X2¼ WIRED UZ TO WATCH OUT FOR!
YEZ. HE IZ THE ONLY ONE WHAT GOT OFF ZE TRAIN AT ZE STATION.

YOO-HOO, GENERAL! ZE CHAMBER OF COMMERCE ZENT UZ TO MEET YOU. ZEY ARE PLANNING A REZEPTION FOR YOU. WON'T YOU STEP INTO ZE CAR?
ZEY DID! ZEY ARE! ZE GOOD OLD CHAMBER! I KNEW ZEY WOULDN'T LET ME DOWN!

YOU FOOL! THAT RECEPTION IS FOR THE REAL GENERAL, NOT YOU!
I KNOW. BUT FIRST THINGS FIRST, OLD BOY. WE GIVE THE GENERAL THE SLIP NOW AND WORRY THEN!

ZEY ACT WERRY PECULIAR. ZE GENERAL AND HIZ AIDE.
ZAT IZ TRUE. BUT WASHINGTON IZ ZMART! ZEY THINK NO ONE WOULD ZUZPECT ZUCH A GENERAL WOULD BE CARRYING ZE ZECRET FORMULA!

...AND TWENTY MINUTES LATER...
TUNNEL OF LOVE
SAY, THIS IS A FUNNY PLACE FOR THE CHAM-BER OF COMMERCE.
GOOD! ZEY ARE NOT ZUZPICIOUS. WE WILL TAKE THEM THE ZECRET WAY TO OUR AGENT.

ZIS IS ONLY A SHORT CUT TO ZE CHAMBER OF COMMERCE.
YOU MEAN WE GO THROUGH THE TUNNEL OF LOVE TO GET TO THE CHAMBER OF COMMERCE? OH, BOY! AM I GOING TO LOVE THIS!
IT LOOKS FISHY TO ME!

THERE'S SOME-THING PHONY GOING ON!
OUT WITH THE ANCHOR!
DON'T PAY ANY ATTENTION TO HIM, HONEY. HE'S JUST JEALOUS!

UGH!
STOP UGHING, ABBOTT. YOU SOUND LIKE AN INDIAN!
KLUNK!

THIS IS THE MOST BEAUTIFUL SCENERY I'VE EVER SEEN. LET'S DROP ANCHOR AND STAY HERE A FEW DAYS.
BUT ZE CHAMBER OF COMMERCE!

ZEY ARE WAITING FOR YOU, YOU BIG, HANDSOME GENERAL!
LET 'EM WAIT! LET 'EM WAIT! PUT ON THE BRAKES, ABBOTT! DIDJA HEAR ME?

YOUR AIDE HIT HIZ HEAD ON ZE ZEILING! HE IZ TEMPORARILY BLACKED OUT, GENERAL!
LUCKY STIFF! I WISH WE WERE STILL BLACKED OUT. IT WAS SO NICE AND COZY IN THERE.

WELL, LET'S GET THE RECEPTION OVER SO WE CAN GO BACK TO THE TUNNEL OF LOVE, HONEY. SAY--I DON'T EVEN KNOW YOUR NAME!

MY NAME IZ MADAME XYZ 2.
SEEING AS I'M A FRIEND OF YOURS, I'LL JUST CALL YOU MADAME X.
FFICE

OHH! WHAT HIT ME? I FEEL LIKE THE CEILING FELL IN ON MY HEAD!
YOU WERE JUST HIT BY THE TUNNEL OF LOVE, ABBOTT, OLD BEAN.

I PINCHED THIZ WALLET OUT OF ZE GENERAL'S POCKET, AGENT 1. IZ THE FORMULA INZIDE?
NO! NUZZING IN HERE BUT ZOME PICTURES OF WIFE AND ZE BABY AND ZE BABY'S DIET.

ZE GENERAL MUST HAVE ZE FORMULA MEMORIZED IN HIZ HEAD. LEAVE HIM ALONE WITH ME. I WILL WORM IT OUT OF ZE SNAKE!

HEY! WHERE'S THE ONE-MAN CHAMBER OF COMMERCE GOING?
I TOLD HIM WE WANTED TO BE ALONE!

SORRY, ABBOTT, CHUM... BUT YOU HEARD THE LADY. SHE AND I WANT TO BE ALONE.

THIZ CONFEZZIONS PERFUME WILL MAKE ZE GENERAL TELL ALL!

I DON'T MIND TELLING YOU, MADAME X, I'VE FALLEN FOR YOU... OOOPS!!

LOOK OUT, GENERAL! ZE PERFUME!

M-M-M... NOW I'M PROBABLY THE SWEETEST SMELLING SOLDIER IN THE U.S. ARMY, AND THAT GOES FOR THE WAC'S, TOO!
I CAN'T REZIZT ZE CONFEZZIONS PERFUME! NO ONE CAN! I MUST TELL YOU ZE TRUTH!

FOOLISH MAIDEN! WHAT IS THERE TO TELL? I LOVE IRRESISTABLE YOU. YOU LOVE IRRESISTABLE I.

FOOL! I HATE ZE! BUT I CAN'T REZIST ZE! AND...

...I AM A ZECRET AGENT FOR ZE ENEMY. WHEN WE GET ZE ZECRET FORMULA FROM YOU, WE KILL YOU!

ABBOTT! ABBOTT!! I KNOW A SECRET!
SWISH!

A FINE KETTLE OF FISH YOU GOT US INTO! WHAT DID YOU DO TO GET HER SO MAD?
NOTHING! THEY'RE ENEMY AGENTS! THEY'RE TRYING TO GET A SECRET I'M SUPPOSED TO KNOW!
THE MAD PURSUIT RAGES IN AND OUT, UP AND DOWN, OVER AND UNDER THE AMUSEMENT PARK...
HURRY, COSTELLO!
B-BUT, I'M AFRAID OF SHOOT-THE-SHOOTS!
A-ABBOTT!! DO YOU THINK THAT GUN'S LOADED!
I THINK THEY'RE GAINING ON US! HIHO, SILVER!
RUN, COSTELLO, RUN!
BELIEVE ME, THIS IS THE FIRST TIME I EVER RAN AWAY FROM A WOMAN!
LOOK, COSTELLO! THEY'RE GAINING ON US!
FINALLY, THE SINISTER PURSUERS HAVE ABBOTT AND COSTELLO CORNERED IN THE HOUSE OF FUN!
Y-YOU MEAN THERE'S NO EXIT HERE? IT'S A FIRE HAZARD!
A FIRING LINE HAZARD, YOU MEAN!
HERE THEY COME!

WE KNOW YOU HAVE ZE FORMULA. OUR AGENT X2¼ OVERHEARD YOU TELL YOUR WIFE YOU HAD IT WHEN YOU BOARDED THE TRAIN. TELL IT TO UZ OR WE'LL SHOOT YOU!

ABBOTT, STAND ON THE OTHER SIDE! MAKE THEM WASTE AN EXTRA BULLET!
L-LOOK! ISN'T THAT THE GENERAL WHO BELONGS TO YOUR COAT?

HA! I CAUGHT UP WITH YOU! I SPOTTED YOU WHEN YOU LEFT THE PARKING LOT!
BOY, GENERAL! AM I GLAD YOU'RE PART BLOODHOUND!

STOP THEM! THEY'RE ENEMY AGENTS!

COME OVER HERE, YOU CROOKS AND TAKE A GOOD WHIFF OF MY CONFESSION'S PERFUME. THEN TELL THE GENERAL ALL ABOUT YOURSELVES!

HMM... I SUPPOSE I MUST BE LENIENT WITH YOU AND FORGET ABOUT YOUR STEALING MY JACKET. WHAT WERE THOSE SPIES AFTER ANYWAY?
THE SECRET FORMULA YOU TOLD YOUR WIFE YOU HAD, OF COURSE!

HA-HA!! THEIR AGENTS OVERHEARD ME AND THOUGHT I WAS TALKING ABOUT A SECRET FORMULA! I WAS TALKING ABOUT OUR LITTLE BABY'S MILK FORMULA.
WHAT A BUNCH OF PUDDING-HEADS, GENERAL!
P.
END

ABBOTT AND COSTELLO

in Seen But Not Heard

SO WHAT IF YOU DID SPEND FIVE HOURS FIXING THE HATS? I TELL YOU A LADY WANTS TO **BUY** ONE!

NO! NO! **NO!**

SOME MINUTES LATER...
THE DUMMY FOR THE DARE-DEVIL ACT ON THE SKYSCRAPER? HELP YOURSELF. THE MODELS ARE IN THE REAR!
THANKS, BUD.

HERE'S A DOPEY LOOKING DUMMY. YOU'D THINK THEY WOULD MAKE THEM MORE LIFELIKE WOULDN'T YOU?
MAYBE HE'S A MODEL FOR ONE OF THEM TOY PARADE BALLOONS!

SAY, MAYBE HE IS A BALLOON!
NAW— LOOK! WHEN I JAB HIM WITH THIS HAT-PIN HE DON'T BURST!
AH-AH, LOU— REMEMBER! TEN DOLLARS!

WE'LL TAKE THIS ONE, THEN!
HEY - BE CAREFUL. WE MIGHT BREAK HIM!
THUDDDD!

AWWW, WHAT COULD HURT HIM? HE'S JUST A DUMMY. LOOK!
YEAH, I SEE WHAT YOU MEAN.
MOVERS
POWWWW!

CRAAASSSH!
CLANNNGGG!
HEAVE! HO!
OKAY, THEN. LET'S GO!

MEANWHILE...
WONDER WHICH DUMMY THOSE WORKMEN TOOK? HMMM... THEY ALL SEEM TO BE HERE.

MAYBE LOU KNOWS. HEY-Y-Y, COSTELLO!

LOU! LOU! WHERE ARE YOU? ANSWER ME! HE-HE'S **GONE**!

GONE? OH, NO! COSTELLO **LOOKS** LIKE A DUMMY— BUT STILL... I'D BETTER MAKE SURE!

At THAT MOMENT...
BOY, I WANT A FRONT ROW SEAT WHEN THE PROFESSOR DROPS THIS DUMMY SEVENTY STORIES TO THE STREET!
ME, TOO!

DID YOU SAY SOMETHIN', JOE?
NO. FUNNY, I THOUGHT **YOU** DID!
MMMBBFFGGGBB...

HERE, PROFESSOR! HERE'S THAT DUMMY YOU ORDERED.
JUST DROP HIM ANYWHERE, BOYS!

THERE! THE WIRE IS ALL RIGHT. NOW TO TAKE THE DUMMY WHILE THE CROWD IS WATCHING AND—DROP HIM. IT'LL BE GREAT PUBLICITY FOR THE CIRCUS!

ONE OR TWO MORE STEPS AND— I'LL LET HIM FALL!
LEE ST.
MAIN ST.

HMMM... A LITTLE HEAVIER THAN I ANTICIPATED, BUT THAT ONLY MEANS THAT HE'LL **BOUNCE** HIGHER!

HEY, COSTELLO! WHAT ARE YOU DOING THERE, YOU SHOWOFF? I TURN MY BACK FOR AN HOUR AND THIS IS WHERE YOU GO!
AN HOUR? THEN THAT HALF-HOUR IS UP! I CAN TALK AGAIN!

HELP!
HELP!

I CAN'T LOOK!
YEEEOOOOW!

CATCH HOLD! I'LL HAVE YOU SAFE IN A JIFFY!
LET GO OF MY FOOT, YOU IDIOT!
ARE YOU KIDDING??

MY TEN BUCKS! WHERE'S THE TEN BUCKS I EARNED BY KEEPING QUIET, ABBOTT? I SURE EARNED IT. BOY, WHAT I WENT THROUGH!
HERE, HERE! TAKE THE TEN. I ONLY HOPE YOU LEARNED YOUR LESSON! JUST KEEP QUIET AND YOU'LL NEVER GET INTO TROUBLE!

REMEMBER, NOW. DON'T YELL OR SHOUT. THAT'S RUDE! JUST SPEAK MODERATELY!
WELL, IF YOU INSIST!

COSTELLO, WHY DIDN'T YOU YELL AND WARN ME THAT TRUCK WAS SO CLOSE?
IT'S RUDE TO YELL, ABBOTT. YOU SAID SO YOURSELF!

TO BE OR NOT TO BE ???

WHAT'S THE USE ?

LOU COSTELLO
in
"The MODEL MALE"

MALE
MODEL
WANTED

SUITS

SUITS

HATS-

MANAGER
MALE MODELS
APPLY HERE

PHOTO STUDIO→

CLKK!

TWO WEEKS LATER . . .

ABBOTT! ABBOTT! I'M FAMOUS. I'M MADE!
MY PICTURE'S IN THE PAPER!

YOU MEAN THEY REALLY PRINTED **YOUR** PICTURE?
YEAH, LOOK!

WHITEHALL
COLLARS
FIT EVEN THE FATTEST NECKS!
END

ABBOTT and COSTELLO

IN

"TROPICAL TRAPPERS"

GOSH, ABBOTT! I CAN HARDLY BELIEVE WE'RE IN *COSTA GUAVA!*

I STILL WISH WE WERE *BACK HOME!*

YIPE!
BANG!
BANG!
BANG!

EEE-III!!
BANG!
BANG!
BANG!

WH-WHO WAS THAT?
COSTA GUAVA IS PLAGUED BY THREE THINGS... FLOODS, HURRICANES, AND...

...EL PANCHO AND HEES BANDITS!
THAT WAS EL PANCHO?

MEANWHILE...
THERE EET EES, EL PANCHO!
I WEEL TAKE CARE OF HEEM!
EL PANCHO CASINO
PEDRO
EL PANCHO'S

YOU ARE PEDRO, THE FORMER OWNER OF THEES PLACE?
ULP I-I AM PEDRO, THE PRESENT OWNER OF THEES PLACE!
SALE

I, EL PANCHO, OWN EVERY SHOP ON THEES STREET BUT YOURS!
S-S-SI!
SAL

YOU ARE THE FORMER OWNER OF THEES PLACE! UNDERSTAND?
S-S-SI, EL PANCHO!

I'LL GEEV YOU TILL TOMORROW TO GET OUT OF TOWN!
S-SI, EL PANCHO!
PEDRO

WE OUGHTA OPEN UP A LITTLE BUSINESS!
IT LOOKS LIKE EL PANCHO HAS THE TOWN SEWED UP!
EL PANCHO CLOTHES
EL PANCHO NIGHT CLUB
EL PANC GRILL

HEY! LOOK! A PLACE THAT DOESN'T BELONG TO EL PANCHO!
LET'S GO IN!
PEDRO

WOULD YOU LIKE TO SELL THIS PLACE?
WOULD I?
HE SEEMS TOO ANXIOUS!

YOU CAN HAVE EET FOR A HUNDRED PASAVOS!
GOSH! THAT'S ONLY TEN DOLLARS IN AMERICAN MONEY!

HOW COME YOU'RE SO EAGER TO SELL?
EET EES A MATTER OF HEALTH. EET WOULD BE UNHEALTHY FOR ME TO STAY HERE!
IT'S A DEAL!

ADIOS, SENORS! AND GOOD LUCK!
THERE'S SOMETHING SCREWY ABOUT THIS!

THE ONLY THING SCREWY AROUND HERE IS YOU! AND I EVEN FOUND A GARMENT HERE FOR YOU!

A STRAIT-JACKET!
GOSH! THIS PLACE HAS EVERYTHING FROM SOUP TO NUTS!

I'M GONNA GET A NEW SIGN MADE... "GENERAL STORE"!
GOOD IDEA!

GENERAL STORE

EL PANCHO! EL PANCHO!
WHAT EES EET, SNEAKY PETE?

A GENERAL HAS TAKEN OVER PEDRO'S SHOP!
A GENERAL?

SI! SOME GENERAL BY THE NAME OF STORE!
GENERAL OR NO GENERAL, NO-BODY'S GOING TO MUSCLE IN ON EL PANCHO! COME ON, BOYS!

WAIT FOR ME HERE!
SI, EL PANCHO!
GENERAL STORE

WHEECH ONE OF YOU EES THE GENERAL!
ULP

HIM!
HIM!
WISE HOMBRE, EH?

WE'LL SEE HOW WISE YOU ARE FULL OF LEAD!
ULP

KLUNK!

AMBULANCE! AMBULANCE!
EL PANCHO MUST'VE MOBILIZED THE FAT ONE!
HEH, HEH!

I CAN'T WAIT TO SEE THEM CARRY OUT THE PIECES!
HEH, HEH!
GEN

ULP EET'S EL PANCHO!
WHA..?

EL PANCHO! WHA'HOPPEN?
I WAS DOUBLE-CROSSED! LET ME OUT OF HERE!

I GUESS THAT TAKES CARE OF EL PANCHO!
LOOK, COSTELLO! A TRAP-DOOR!

GOSH! MORE STOCK!
WE SURE BOUGHT A BARGAIN!

ALL RIGHT, BOYS! FILL THE PLACE FULL OF HOLES!

BANG!
BANG!
BANG!
BANG!
BANG!
BANG!
BANG!

EEF THERE'S ANYTHING LEFT OF THOSE HOMBRES, EET'S A MIRACLE!
THEY MUST BE AS FULL OF HOLES AS A SWISS CHEESE!

GOSH! LOOK AT ALL THE BULLET HOLES ALL OVER THE PLACE!
WERE WE LUCKY TO BE DOWNSTAIRS!

OH-OH! HERE COMES EL PANCHO, AGAIN!
ULP

YOU-YOU ARE ALIVE?
NO THANKS TO YOU, I'M SURE!

HOW--HOW DID YOU DO EET?
HUH? OH--ER--WE WORE BULLET-PROOF JACKETS!

BULLET-PROOF JACKETS? WONDERFUL!
SURE! CALL IN YOUR BOYS! I'LL SHOW YOU HOW IT WORKS!

YOU'RE NOT ANGRY?
AHHH! WHAT'S A FEW BULLETS BETWEEN FRIENDS?

WHAT'S THE ANGLE, COSTELLO?
QUICK, ABBOTT! BRING OUT THE STRAIT-JACKETS!

NOW, EACH OF YOU PUT ON ONE OF THESE JACKETS!
BULLET-PROOF JACKETS! TERRIFIC!

TIE 'EM UP GOOD, ABBOTT!
GOSH! YOU CAN HARDLY MOVE EEN THESE THINGS!

NOW WHAT?
NOW, MY STUPID FRIENDS-- OFF TO THE HOOSEGOW!

WHAT?
WE'RE TRAPPED!
YOU HEARD ME, EL PANCHO! COME ON!

LOOK! IT'S EL PANCHO! THEY HAVE CAPTURED EL PANCHO!
CARAMBA!
SACRÉ BLEU!
OY!
NO COMMENT!

AS CHIEF OF POLICE, I WANT TO THANK YOU FOR YOUR MAGNIFICENT CAPTURE OF EL PANCHO AND HIS GANG!
YOU'RE QUITE WELCOME, CHIEF!

I HAVE PROMISED A GREAT REWARD TO THE CAPTOR OF EL PANCHO... THE HAND OF MY BEAUTIFUL DAUGHTER IN MARRIAGE!
HUH?

♫ ANNA! ♫
AHEM!

SI, PAPA?
ULP

I GOTTA GO BACK TO MY DOCTOR FOR ANOTHER PRESCRIPTION!
(PUFF-PUFF) HEY, PAAVO NURMI--SLOW DOWN! YOU'RE SAFE NOW!
THE END

ABBOTT and COSTELLO in TEPEE TOWN
I'VE ALWAYS WANTED TO VISIT AN INDIAN RESERVATION!
ARE--ARE YOU SURE IT'S SAFE, ABBOTT?
INDIAN RESERVATION

SAFE? OF COURSE IT'S SAFE! THE DAYS WHEN INDIANS WERE SAVAGES ARE GONE! TODAY, MANY OF THEM ARE COLLEGE GRADUATES!
NO KIDDING?

TAKE THAT OLD BRAVE, THERE--I WOULDN'T BE SURPRISED IF HE SPEAKS LATIN AND GREEK!
GEE--

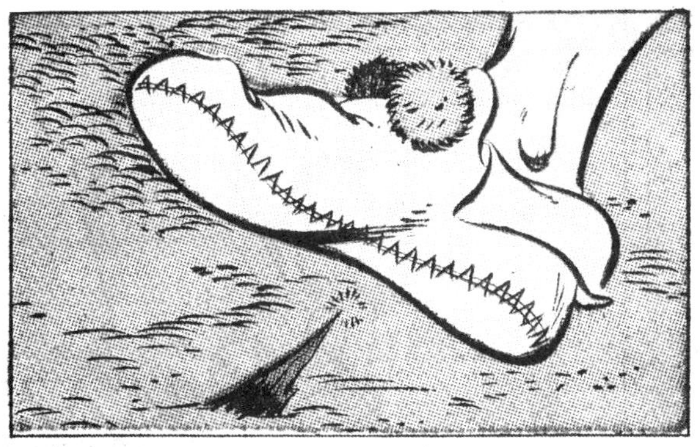

YI-I-I!

HELP!
?

HIM--I GUESS THERE ARE STILL A FEW WILD ONES AROUND!
GOSH! WHAT A BLOOD THIRSTY YELL!

L-LET'S GET OUTTA HERE, ABBOTT!
COME, COME, COSTELLO! LET'S NOT BE FRIGHTENED AWAY BY ONE GRUDGE-BEARING INDIAN! I'M SURE THE MAJORITY OF THEM ARE CIVILIZED!

BE PREPARED FOR THE, CRUMPLED-PETAL! TWO OF THOSE CRAZY TOURISTS ARE PROWLING AROUND!
OH, DEAR!
TOURISTS! TOURISTS!

AS FOR ME, I'M GOING TO LIE DOWN AND TAKE A NAP! I DON'T WANT TO HAVE TO HEAR ANY OF THEIR SILLY QUESTIONS!
YOU'RE LUCKY YOU'RE SUCH A HEAVY SLEEP-ER, BROKEN-TWIG!

HAVE YOU GOT THE KETCHUP, TADPOLE?
RIGHT, LITTLE-SQUIRT! AND YOU HAVE THE RUBBER DAGGER!

HE'S ASLEEP, ALL RIGHT!
POUR SOME KETCHUP ON THE DAGGER, TOO!

OKAY, LITTLE-SQUIRT! HERE THEY COME!
WAIT TILL I LOOSEN HIS TOUPEE!

SEEMS QUIET ENOUGH AROUND HERE!
YEAH, NICE AND PEACEFUL!

A-A-A-A-A-A-A!

WH-WHAT WAS THAT??
IT...IT SOUNDED LIKE MURDER!

HE'S DEAD ALL RIGHT!
GOOD RIDDANCE
ULP!

NOW TO SCALP HIM
OH, NO!
AHH!

STOP IT! STOP IT, YOU KIDS!

HA!
OOOOHHH!

WHAT HAVE YOU KIDS DONE? THIS IS HORRIBLE!
WHAT EVER MADE YOU DO A THING LIKE THAT?
WE JUST DIDN'T LIKE HIM!

I'M GONNA TELL THE CHIEF! WHERE'S THE CHIEF OF THIS TRIBE?
CHIEF!
SNITCHERS!

CHIEF! CHIEF! WHERE'S THE CHIEF?
IN BIG WIGWAM!
SCREECH!

CHIEF! A COUPLE OF LITTLE INDIAN BOYS JUST MURDERED A MAN AND SCALPED HIM!

BROKEN-TWIG'S KIDS AGAIN...

HA! HA HA HA HA HA HA
HA HA HA HA HA HA HA!
HA HA HA!
?
?

THEY THINK IT'S FUNNY!
WH-WHAT A SENSE OF HUMOR!

LET'S HAVE SOME FUN WITH THESE GUYS!
HEH, HEH, HEH!

HOW!
HUH? OH, HOW!
HOW!

YOU WHITE MEN?
ER...Y-YES, SIR!
OF COURSE WE HAVE A GREAT RESPECT FOR OUR RED BROTHERS!

WHY YOU STEAL COUNTRY FROM RED MAN?
WE WEREN'T EVEN IN ON THE DEAL!
I WAS AGAINST IT!

WHITE MAN MUST DIE!
CHIEF! DON'T TALK CRAZY! WE HAD NOTHING TO DO WITH IT!
YEAH, WE WERE AGAINST IT!

GRAB THEM!
SORRY CHIEF WE'VE GOT TO BE GOING!
'BYE!

HA, HA, HA, HA, HA, HA, HA, HA, HA HA!
THEY'RE THE LAUGHINGEST INDIANS IN CAPTIVITY!
THEY MUST BE DESCENDANTS OF MINE--HA-HA!

OOWW!
HEY! THAT AIN'T LAUGHTER!
WHAT TH--!

LOOK!
HEY!

THE MURDERED INDIAN SPANKING THE KIDS!
AND HE'S GOT HIS SCALP BACK!

WHATEVER ELSE IS WRONG WITH THIS SCREWY TRIBE...
...THEY'VE GOT THE GREATEST MEDICINE MAN IN THE WORLD!
YOU AIN'T KIDDING!
INDIAN RESERVATION
THE END

ABBOTT AND COSTELLO COMICS
THAT GUY SYNCOPATES HIS SHOTS! I LIKE WALTZ TIME BETTER!
By
10 CENTS
No. 1

ABBOTT and COSTELLO

in

"BENT BUT NOT BROKE"

WHAT'S THE MATTER WITH YOU, COSTELLO? ARE YOU STILL LOOKING FOR THAT *DIME* YOU DROPPED THREE DAYS AGO?

I'M NOT *LOOKING* FOR ANYTHING. I JUST *CAN'T STRAIGHTEN UP!*

WOW! LOOK AT THAT PRETTY GIRL UP THERE!
WHERE?

SLIP!

BAW! WHAT'RE YOU TRYIN' TO DO TO ME, ABBOTT?
GEE, THIS IS SERIOUS!

COME ON! WE'D BETTER SEE DOCTOR HERMAN!
N...NO! WAIT! M...MAYBE IT WILL GO AWAY!

COME ON! DON'T BE SUCH A BABY!
BUT HE MAY WANT TO OPERATE!

IF I DIE ON THE OPERATING TABLE, ABBOTT, I'LL NEVER FORGIVE YOU!
I'M WILLING TO TAKE THAT CHANCE!
DR. HERMAN

OH, MR. COSTELLO! YOU DON'T HAVE TO BOW TO LITTLE OLD ME!
I'M NOT BOWING!
CAN WE SEE DR. HERMAN?

RIGHT THIS WAY, MR. COSTELLO!
GULP!
G-GOOD LUCK LOU!

WELL! HOW DO YOU DO, MR. COSTELLO? WHY THE EXAGERATED POLITENESS?
I'M NOT BEING POLITE, DR. HERMAN! I JUST CAN'T STRAIGHTEN UP!

AND HOW LONG HAVE YOU HAD THIS CONDITION?
SINCE THIS MORNING!

HM! DID YOU HURT YOUR BACK OR STRAIN YOURSELF?
NO, SIR! I DON'T FEEL ANY PAIN!
VERY STRANGE!

LET ME HELP YOU OFF WITH YOUR COAT AND...

..NOW THE SHIRT... AHH!

HAW, HAW, HAW! I'LL HAVE YOU STRAIGHTENED OUT IN A JIFFY!
?

WE'LL JUST TAKE HOLD, HERE, AND..
HEE, HEE! STOP, DOC! YOU'RE TICKLING ME!

I'M CURED! I'M STANDING STRAIGHT! HOW DID YOU DO IT, DOC? WHAT WAS THE MATTER?
VERY SIMPLE, MR. COSTELLO! HEH, HEH!

YOU HAD YOUR SHIRT BUTTONED TO THE SUSPENDER BUTTONS ON YOUR TROUSERS!

HOW DOPEY CAN YOU GET! DOC, YOU WON'T TELL ABBOTT ABOUT THIS, WILL YA?
WHAT GOES ON BETWEEN A PATIENT AND A DOCTOR IS STRICTLY PRIVATE! WHILE YOU'RE HERE WE'LL GIVE YOU A THOROUGH CHECK-UP! TAKE OFF YOUR SHIRT!

DOCTOR! WILL YOU LOOK AT THOSE X-RAYS?
EXCUSE ME, MR. COSTELLO!
SURE, DOC!

HOW DO YOU DO? DIDN'T YOU POSE FOR THE LABELS ON THE IODINE BOTTLES?

DOCTOR HERMAN
ULP! WHERE'S MY SHIRT?

I HOPE THE DOC DOESN'T MIND IF I BORROW ONE OF HIS!

DOCTOR HERMAN, I'M A VERY SICK LITTLE GIRL!
WOW! WHEN I SAY THERE'S NOTHING WRONG WITH YOU... I'M NOT KIDDING!

BUT THERE IS! I FEEL LAZY AND TIRED...NO PEP OR AMBITION!
GOSH! THAT SOUNDS LIKE MY UNCLE NED!

DO YOU WANT TO LOOK AT MY TONGUE?
MIGHT AS WELL! I HAVE NOTHING ELSE TO DO!

YIPE!

QUICK! WE'VE GOT TO GET YOU TO A HOSPITAL!
WHAT IS IT?!

YOUR TONGUE IS BLACK AS COAL!
BLACK? OH, YES! I FORGOT!

I HAD A LICORICE DROP JUST BEFORE I CAME IN!
LADY...I CAN'T TAKE TOO MUCH OF THIS!

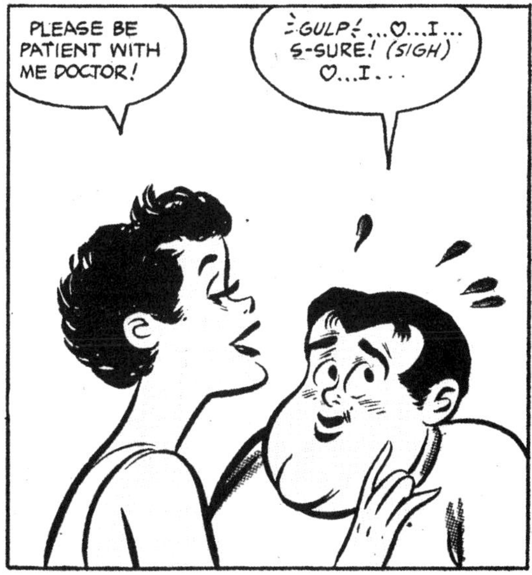
PLEASE BE PATIENT WITH ME DOCTOR!
GULP! ...♡...I... S-SURE! (SIGH) ♡...I...

IS MY PULSE NORMAL?
I DON'T KNOW ABOUT YOURS... BUT... MINE AIN'T!

SIT DOWN! I ALWAYS LIKE TO GET COMFORTABLE WHEN I'M TAKING A PATIENT'S PULSE!
THANK YOU!

DOCTOR, YOU'VE BEEN HOLDING MY HAND FIVE MINUTES! HAVEN'T YOU GOTTEN THE COUNT YET?
FIVE MINUTES? SEEMS LIKE ONLY FIVE SECONDS!

SAY WHAT'S THE MATTER WITH YOU? ARE YOU A DOCTOR OR AREN'T YOU?
I NEVER SAID I WAS!

COSTELLO! WHAT ARE YOU UP TO?
FAKE!

I'LL HAVE YOU LOCKED UP FOR IMPERSONATING A DOCTOR!
PHONEY!

QUICK, ABBOTT! LET'S SCRAM!
COSTELLO! YOU'RE STRAIGHT-ENED OUT!

YEAH! BUT I'M AFRAID I'LL GET BENT AGAIN IF WE DON'T HURRY!
DOCTOR HERMAN
END

ABBOTT and COSTELLO in MAN IN UNIFORM

AND NOW A FEW WORDS FROM OUR HERO OF THE WEEK.

GET UP OUTA YOUR CHAIR, STUPID. YA GOTTA MAKE A **SHORT** SPEECH.

ABBOTT... SOME DAY I'M GONNA...
GO ON WITH THE SPEECH.

MEN...
THAT'S LONG ENOUGH. YOUR SPEECH TIME IS UP.

GEE...ME IN A UNIFORM. AN' LEADER OF A TROOP FOR A WHOLE WEEK... BOY!
THAT'S BECAUSE YA COLLECTED THE MOST NEWSPAPERS FOR THE BOYSCOUT DRIVE.

AHEM NOW THAT YOU'RE THE EAGLE OF THE WEEK...
HEY, ABBOTT, WHAT'S THIS GUY TALKIN' ABOUT? FIRST I'M A BOYSCOUT AND NOW I'M AN EAGLE.

AN "EAGLE" IS A LEADER OF A TROOP, STUPID. SHUT UP AND LISTEN.

CONGRATULATIONS "EAGLE" COSTELLO.
GO OUT THERE AND SHAKE HANDS WITH YOUR TROOP, STUPID.

WOW! YA MEAN I HAVE TO SHAKE ALL THEIR HAND?
YES.
TROOP 79

•4,000 HANDSHAKES LATER...
NOW YA GOTTA PROVE TO YOUR TROOP THAT YOU'RE A WORTHY LEADER!
OHH MY HAND!

WHAT DO YOU MEAN, WORTHY LEADER?
FIRST, YA GOTTA DO AT LEAST ONE GOOD DEED A DAY. C'MON AND I'LL SHOW YA!

OKAY!
SEE THAT OLD LADY THAT JUST DROPPED HER HAND-BAG. GO PICK IT UP FOR HER.

AH...EXCUSE ME, LADY!
MY HANDBAG!

OF ALL THE SNEAKY NERVE.
KUNK!

HELP...POLICE...THIEF... PURSE SNATCHER!

WHAT'S UP, LADY?
HE TOOK MY HANDBAG!
I ONLY TOOK HER HANDBAG BECAUSE...

...YA GOT THE HABIT. WELL, MAY-BE THIS'LL HELP YA CHANGE YOUR WAYS!
OUCH! HEY ABBOTT!

JUST A MINUTE, OFFICER. I CAN EXPLAIN EVERYTHING.
HURRY UP BEFORE HE SHAKES ME APART.

OOOOH, THAT COP WAS ROUGH. I'M STILL SHAKING. I DON'T THINK I LIKE THIS GOOD DEED BUSINESS.
SHUT UP. YOU HAVEN'T DONE YOUR GOOD DEED YET. AH, HERE'S ANOTHER CHANCE FOR YOU.

SEE THAT OLD MAN COMING OUTA THE STORE WITH THOSE PACKAGES? GO HELP HIM.
OKAY. THIS IS EASY. THEY'RE SMALL PACKAGES.

I'M A "BIRD" BOY SCOUT, SIR. MAY I HELP YOU WITH YOUR PACKAGES?
SURE.

HEY, I THOUGHT YOU HAD A COUPLE OF PACKAGES.
STEADY YOURSELF, BOY. JUST A FEW MORE.

HEY! WAIT A MINUTE!
I'LL CARRY THIS OTHER PACKAGE. JUST FOLLOW ME.
PHEW!

HURRY, BOY, I'M LATE.
YOU HEARD THE MAN, STUPID. GET A MOVE ON!

THESE GIFTS ARE RUINED, I DEMAND PAYMENT FOR THE DAMAGES.
HE'S GOT YOU LEGALLY, LOU... YOU'LL HAVE TO PAY HIM.

FORTY DOLLARS! BUT I ONLY SMASHED SIX PACKAGES.
THEY WERE THE EX-PENSIVE PACKAGES.
PAY THE MAN, LOU.

FORTY DOLLARS IS CORRECT, AND HERE'S TWENTY FOR YOU.
THANK YOU, SIR
HEY. JUST A MINUTE!

THAT GOOD DEED COST ME FORTY BUCKS AN' YOU JUST GOT TWENTY OF IT, HOW COME?
I WAS A WITNESS.
YOU SHOULD'VE BEEN MY WITNESS.

OKAY, I'LL BE YOUR WITNESS. GIVE ME TWENTY DOLLARS.
HERE'S TWENTY. GEE, ABBOTT, YOU'RE A REAL PAL.

WAIT A MINUTE. SOMETHING DOESN'T FIGURE OUT RIGHT. I JUST GAVE YOU TWENTY...

FORGET THAT. OUR PROBLEM IS TO HAVE YOU DO A GOOD DEED.
YEAH. BUT WITH LESS EXPENSE AND PUNISHMENT.
HELP!

A BABY BUGGY RACING DOWN THE STREET AND HEADING FOR THE WATERFRONT! AFTER IT, LOU!
RIGHT! I WON'T FAIL THIS TIME!

DON'T WORRY, LADY. MY BUDDY'LL SAVE YOUR BABY!
I DON'T HAVE A BABY. THAT WAS JUST MY SHOPPING BUGGY. IT JUST HAD A SACK OF CEMENT IN IT.

GADS. AND COSTELLO CAN'T SWIM A SINGLE STROKE! HEY, LOU!

PUFF PUFF I'M GAINING. I'LL SAVE THE LITTLE GUY IF IT'S THE LAST THING I DO.

HEY, ABBOTT! HOW D'YA PUT THE BRAKES ON THESE THINGS!

ABBOTT!

BLUB BLUB GIMME A HAND, SOMEBODY. THIS LITTLE GUY IS HEAVY! HALP... BLUB.

HE'S GONE DOWN FOR THE THIRD TIME!
HASN'T COME UP YET.
THERE GOES A BOAT OUT AFTER HIM!

THEY'RE WORKING ON HIM. HE'S STARTING TO COME TO.
LET ME THROUGH, COSTELLO, ARE YOU OKAY?

COSTELLO. SNAP OUT OF IT. ARE YOU OKAY?
CEMENT

BLUB!! I SAVED HIM...I SAVED HIM, ABBOTT... I...AH...
YOU SAVED A SACK OF CEMENT, STUPID!

CEMENT!!
AND YOU STILL HAVEN'T DONE YOUR "GOOD DEED".

THIS DOES IT, ABBOTT. I'M GOING TO...TO...
SHUT UP. YOU'RE NO QUITER, ARE YOU? WHAT'S THAT IN YOUR BACK POCKET?

IT'S A FISH. I CAUGHT IT IN MY BACK POCKET.
SO...FISHING MEANS MORE TO YOU THAN YOUR UNIFORM, EH?

DID I HEAR SOMEONE SAY HE CAUGHT A FISH?
SURE. HE DID.

DO YOU HAVE A FISHING LICENSE, CHUBBY?
NO. WHY?
CEMENT

I'M THE GAME WARDEN AN' YA NEED A LICENSE TO FISH. THAT'LL COST YA FIFTY DOLLARS!
HUH!

FIFTY DOLLARS FOR ONE FISH. I COULDA BOUGHT A WHOLE FISH MARKET FOR THAT MUCH!
FORGET IT. THERE'RE MORE IMPORTANT THINGS FOR YOU TO THINK ABOUT. REMEMBER?

THE WEEK COMES TO AN END..
THIS IS THE LAST DAY, COSTELLO. YOU'VE FAILED TO DO A GOOD DEED.
WHAT'LL I DO, ABBOTT?

GO TURN IN YOUR UNIFORM. I'M DISAPPOINTED IN YOU, COSTELLO.
SIGH WHY DOES THIS SORT OF LUCK HAVE TO HAPPEN TO ME.
BOY SCOUT HEAD QUARTER

DON'T TAKE IT, SO HARD, COSTELLO.
I'D GIVE ANYTHING TO BE ABLE TO WEAR A UNIFORM AGAIN.

COSTELLO, I'VE GOT AN IDEA. HOW'D YOU LIKE TO BE IN THE SERVICE?
YA MEAN A SOLDIER? SAILOR? OR A MARINE?

HUH! COSTELLO!
WELL, NOT EXACTLY.

YOU AND YOUR BRIGHT IDEAS. WHY DIDN'T YOU SAY, "STREET-SERVICE".
The END

ABBOTT and COSTELLO
IN
GROAN AND BEAR IT!
GRRR!
STOP GRUMBLING, ABBOTT! AND PUT MORE BOUNCE BEHIND THE OUNCE!

THERE'S NOTHING LIKE HARD OUTDOOR WORK TO TONE UP YOUR MUSCLES, EH, COSTELLO?
YEAH... I CAN HEAR THEM SCREAMING ALL OFF-KEY!

AHH... AND THIS FRESH CRISP AIR!!
THIS CRISP AIR IS TURNING ME INTO AN ICICLE! I'M GOING TO GET A JACKET!

GRRR!
BACK ALREADY, COSTELLO?

WHERE'D YOU GET THAT CRAZY FUR COAT?
?

WHAT'S THE MATTER WITH YOU, COSTELLO? TRYIN' TO KILL ME? PUSHING THAT SAW IN MY STOMACH!
WHAC!

HEY! YOU'RE NOT COSTELLO! YEOW!
GRRR!

HMM... NOW WHERE'S THAT JACKET?

AHHH... THIS OUGHT TO KEEP ME WARM!

HERE I COME, ABBOTT! I'M READY TO BEAR UP UNDER THIS COLD!

POOR COSTELLO! HE WAS A GOOD FRIEND! HE HAD A HEART AS BIG AS A WHALE... AND THE BLUBBER TO COVER IT!

OKAY, ABBOTT-- BACK TO WORK!
GRR!!

OOF!!

GRRR-
OOFF!
TWO CAN PLAY AT THIS GAME, ABBOTT! AND DON'T GROWL AT ME!

OOOPH!

ENOUGH'S ENOUGH, ABBOTT!

GRRRR!
MMPH!

JUST BECAUSE YOU LOOK LIKE A BEAR, ABBOTT, IS NO REASON TO ACT LIKE ONE!
GRROW!

Y-Y-YOU ARE A BEAR!
GRRR!

I DON'T KNOW HOW YOU DID IT, ABBOTT--BUT I AIN'T WAIT-ING FOR AN EXPLANATION!

GRRRR!

GOOD-BYE, DEAR FRIEND...
OLD BUDDY... PAL...!

POOR COSTELLO! I'LL HAVE TO...
SOB ... GET HIS THINGS TOGETHER... SOB
... AND SEND THEM TO HIS FAMILY!

I HOPE YOU
GET INDIGESTION,
YOU... YOU...
CANNIBAL!

WHAT A MONSTER! HE
EVEN ATE THE BONES!

YOU WERE A SWEET GUY, COSTELLO...
SOB ... YOU MIGHT HAVE SOB BEEN STUPID,
BUT ON YOU IT LOOKED GOOD! SOB

SOB ... YOU WERE A PAL! THAT MONSTER
EVEN ATE YOUR SOCKS--HOLES AND ALL!...
HE'LL GET A GOOD CASE OF HEARTBURN!

YEOW!

THAT'S A PAL FOR YOU! AFTER ALL
THOSE NICE THINGS HE SAID ABOUT ME,
HE WASN'T EVEN GLAD TO SEE ME!
THE END

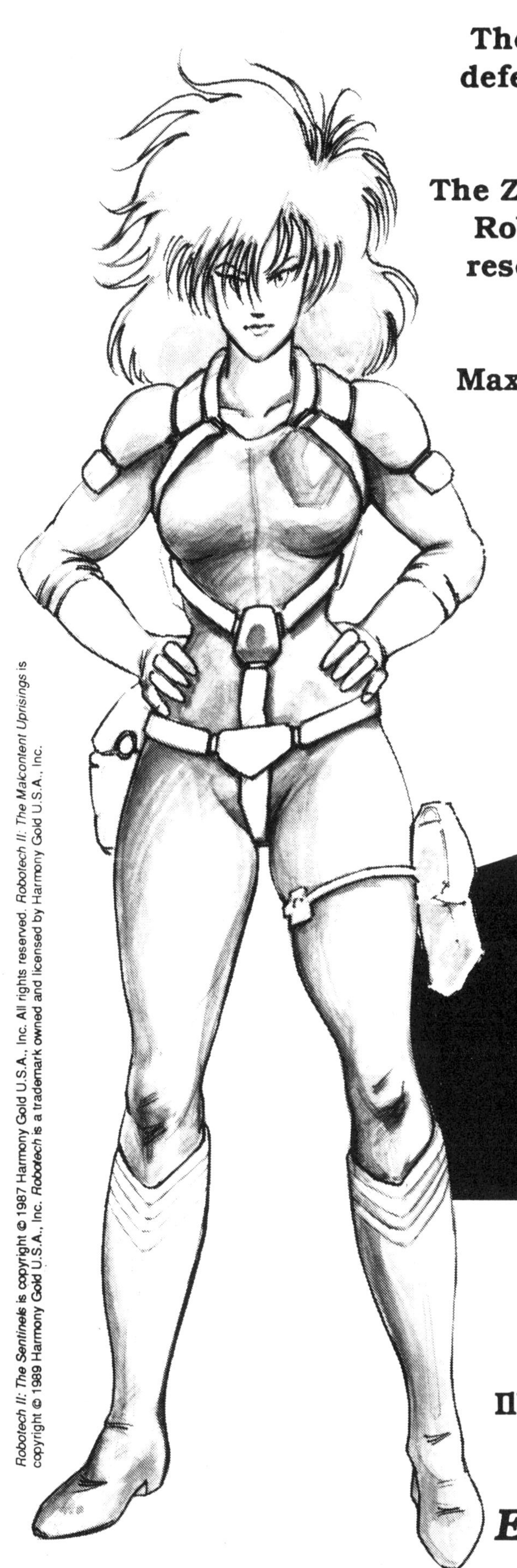

The Robotech Defense Force defeated the Zentraedi at the end of Macross.

The Zentraedi--creations of the Robotech Masters--are being resettled and integrated into society.

Max Sterling has taken as his bride Miriya, a Zentraedi.

The First Robotech War is officially over.

Don't bet on it.

ROBOTECH II: THE MALCONTENT UPRISINGS

An Original *Robotech* Adventure
Written by Bill Spangler
Illustrated by Michael Ling

Coming in August from
ETERNITY COMICS
a division of Malibu Graphics, Inc.

HE WAS THE GUN

SOCIETY PULLED THE TRIGGER...

DINOSAURS FOR HIRE
COMING IN JUNE FROM ETERNITY
GUNS N LIZARDS
A Graphic Novel by
TOM MASON
Illustrated by
Bryon Carson &
Mike Roberts
Cover by Paul Gulacy
GULACY
Dinosaurs For Hire is a trademark of Tom Mason.

NINJA
HIGH
SCHOOL
RE
Created,
Written, and
Illustrated by
BEN DUNN
Every Month From
ETERNITY COMICS
NINJA HIGH SCHOOL is trademarked
and copyright ©1989 Ben Dunn.
BEN
DUNN

ALSO AVAILABLE FROM MALIBU GRAPHICS

Minimum Order: 5 books. All prices include postage (US orders only—Canada and Mexico add $1.00 per order, Overseas add $2.00 per order). Comics are shipped in plastic bags. Send orders and make checks payable to: MALIBU GRAPHICS, PO Box 3185-M, Thousand Oaks, CA 91359

ARGONAUTS
#2-3 $2.50ea

BLADE OF SHURIKEN
#1-5 $1.00ea

BLIND FEAR
Sherlock Holmes returns! All new!
#1-2 $2.50ea

BLOOD BROTHERS
#1-4 $2.50ea

BLOODWING
#1-5 $2.50ea

BUSHIDO
#1-4 $2.50ea

CHARLIE CHAN
World's Greatest Oriental Detective. Strips from the '30s.
#1-3 $2.50ea

CHINA SEA
Graphic Novel
From the creator of *Elflord.*
$7.00

COSMIC HEROES
Buck Rogers, 25th Century A.D. returns to comics in this monthly collection of the classic strip from the '30s.
#1-6 $2.50ea

CRIME CLASSICS
The Shadow returns in this collection of the classic comic strip from the '40s.
#1, 3-7 $2.50ea

DARK WOLF
(Mini-Series)
#1 $6.00
#2-4 $3.00ea
(Regular Series)
#1 $3.00 #2-4, 6-12 $2.50ea
Annual #1 $3.00
Dark Wolf Collection $8.00

DEMON HUNTER
#1-2 $2.50ea
#1 (Signed) $5.00

DINOSAURS FOR HIRE
#1 (2nd print), #2-7 $2.50ea
Fall Classic
#1 $3.00

DRAGONFORCE
#5-8 $2.50ea

EDGAR ALLAN POE
The Pit And The Pendulum $2.50
Mask Of Red Death $2.50
Rue Morgue $2.50
Black Cat $2.50

ELFLORD
#23-27 $2.50ea

EMPIRE
#1-4 $1.00ea

EX-MUTANTS
(Original Series)
#1(Signed by Ron Lim) $10.00 ea
#6-10 $2.50ea

EX-MUTANTS Graphic Novel Volume One: The Saga Begins
96pp. $8.00
Volume Two: Gods Or Men
96pp. $8.00

EX-MUTANTS: The Shattered Earth Chronicles
All new!
#1 $3.00
#2-10 $2.50ea
Annual #1 $3.00
Pin-Up Book #1 $3.00

FIFTIES TERROR
Pre-Code horror from the '50s.
#1-6 $2.50ea

FIST OF GOD
#2-4 $2.50ea

FRANKENSTEIN
All new adaptation of the classic horror novel by Martin Powell and Patrick Olliffe.
#1-2 $2.50ea

FRIGHT
#1-2, 4-9 $2.50ea
#3 (Nightmare On Elm Street cover) $3.00

GUN FURY
He was the gun... society pulled the trigger.
#1-4 $2.50ea
#1 (Signed) $5.00

HOWL
Werewolf tales
#1-2 $2.50ea

HUMAN GARGOYLES
#1-4 $2.50ea

INVISOWORLD
#1 $1.00

KIKU SAN
#1-5 $2.50ea

LIBERATOR
#1-2, 5-6 $2.50 ea

LUNATIC BINGE
Halloween horror.
#1 $1.00

NAZRAT
#6 $1.00

NEW HUMANS Shattered Earth
#2-113 $2.50ea
Annual #1 $3.50

NINJA FUNNIES
#2-5 $1.00ea

NINJA HIGH SCHOOL
All-new adventures by Ben Dunn!
#6-11 $2.50ea
#1 (60 pp) $3.50
#2-3, 3 1/2, 4 $2.50ea
Graphic Novel $9.00
Graphic Novel (signed) $15.00

PRIVATE EYES
The Saint returns in this collection of his '50s strips.
#1-3 $2.50ea
#4 (60 pp) $3.50

PROBE
#2-3 $1.00ea

ROBOTECH II: THE SENTINELS
At last! The sequel to Macross arrives in comic book form. Tom Mason/ Chris Ulm/Jason and John Waltrip.
#1 (2nd printing) #2-6 $2.50ea
Wedding Special #1 $2.50
Full color poster $6.95

SAMURAI
#2-7 $2.50ea

SCARLET IN GASLIGHT Graphic Novel
Collects all four issues of the acclaimed mini-series—complete with rare art.
$8.00

SCIMIDAR
#1 $2.50
#2-3 $2.50ea
Book II #1 $3.00

SHATTERED EARTH
Tales of the Ex-Mutants Universe
#1-7 $2.50ea

SHERLOCK HOLMES
The classic strip from the '50s collected for the first time.
#1 $3.00
2-10 $2.50ea

SHERLOCK HOLMES CASEBOOK
#1-2 $2.50ea

SHURIKEN TEAM-UP
#1 $1.00

SOLO EX-MUTANTS Shattered Earth
#5-6 $2.50ea

SPICY DETECTIVE STORIES
Graphic Novel
The spiciest detective fiction of the '30s, complete with original illustrations.
$8.00

SPICY TALES
Uncensored tales of Bondage, Murder, and Seduction from the '30s.
#1-7 $3.00ea

STREET HEROES 2005
There's a new breed of criminal —Super-Heroes.
#1-2 $2.50ea

TIGER-X
A Soviet invasion has split America in half.
From Ben Dunn, the creator of *Ninja High School.*
#1, 3 $2.50ea

TORRID AFFAIRS
Classic '50s romance.
#1-2 $2.50ea
#3 (60 pp) $3.50

TROUBLE WITH GIRLS
#2-3 $4.00ea
#8-9, 11-14 $2.50ea
Graphic Novel Volume One
$9.00

TWILIGHT AVENGER
He's back! The costumed avenger from the '30s returns in all new adventures by John Wooley and Terry Tidwell
#1,3, 5-6 $2.50ea

VAMPYRES
#1-3 $2.50ea

VERDICT
#1 $3.00
#2-4 $2.50ea

VICTIMS
#1-5 $2.50ea

VIDEO CLASSICS
Here he comes to save the day-- Mighty Mouse!
#1 (60pp) $3.50

WARLOCK 5
#16-22 $2.50ea
Book II #1 $2.50

WARLOCKS
#1 (Special Edition-40 pages) $3.00
#2-7 $2.50ea

WAR OF THE WORLDS
The Aliens have landed in this all-new adaptation of the classic H.G. Wells novel by Scott Finley and Brooks Hagan.
#1-3 $2.50ea

WEREWOLF AT LARGE
All new horror!
#1 $2.50

WILD KNIGHTS Shattered Earth
#1 $3.00
#2-7 $2.50ea

Note: Minimum Order-- 5 Books.

ROBOTECH II THE SENTINELS™

Aboard the SDF-3, Rick Hunter and his bride-to-be Lisa Hayes undertake a dangerous mission to the homeworld of the Robotech Masters. The Robotech Expeditionary Force, with the SDF-3 disguised as a Zentraedi ship, is prepared to meet the Zentraedi creators in peace.

Unfortunately, another race has beaten the REF to the surface of Tirol--The Invid! Led by the Regent, Invid Shocktroopers are tearing the planet apart in a fierce search for the secret of Protoculture--The Flower Of Life.

All New Story! All New Art!
Based on the unproduced ROBOTECH II: The Sentinels television show!
Adapted by Tom Mason and Chris Ulm.
Illustrated by Jason and John Waltrip
On sale now and every month from
ETERNITY COMICS

a division of Malibu Graphics, Inc.